SCILAB
by
EXAMPLE

M. Affouf

Kean University

Contents

|Preface

This book is designed to show how to use the software package Scilab to help students solve problems from linear algebra, calculus, differential equations and graphics.

This manual is organized into seven chapters. The first chapter introduces the general features of Scilab and its basic syntax. The second chapter contains the fundamental commands and Scilab functions of operations on matrices and applications to linear algebra. The third chapter introduces the programming features of Scilab. The fourth and fifth chapters contains a more detailed look at most of the Scilab commands for graphing two and three dimensional plots. The last chapters contains applications to calculus and differential equations and general mathematical problems.

I hope that this guide can contribute to developing mathematical software skills of Scilab and to better student understanding and performance in mathematical problem solving.

Finally, I would appreciate any comments, suggestions, and corrections which can be addressed to the email below.

M. Affouf

maffouf@kean.edu

1 Scilab Basics

1.1 Introduction

Scilab is a widely used and freely distributed mathematical software. Scilab is a high level programming language for technical computing and interactive environment that integrates computation, visualization, and programming. It compromises three main components:

1. Scilab libraries of functions (procedures).

2. Libraries of FORTRAN and C routines. These libraries are mostly available from Netlib.

3. An interpreter which interacts with libraries.

Scilab can be used in

- Technical computing: Mathematical computation, analysis, visualization, and algorithm development

- Industrial research: Signal processing and communications, testing and measurements, image processing

- Education, Science and Engineering

Scilab syntax is capable of manipulating matrices and all operations on matrix algebra. This allows user to solve many technical computing problems, especially those with matrix and vector formulations, in a fraction of the time it would take to write a program in a scalar non interactive languages.

Scilab has evolved over a period of years and currently is developed by a team of dedicated researchers of Scilab Consortium which was created in 2003 by INRIA (the French national institute for research in computer science and control), the Scilab Consortium has joined the Digiteo Foundation in July 2008 and it includes industrials and academics, pursues the ambition of making Scilab the free reference in numerical computation.

Scilab features a family of add-on application-specific solutions called toolboxes. These modules (toolboxes) allow you to learn and apply specialized technology. These modules are made available to Scilab users directly from Scilab console via a new feature named ATOMS (AuTomatic mOdules Management for Scilab).

1.2   Scilab System

The Scilab system consists of five main parts:

1. Development Environment. This is the set of tools and facilities that help you use Scilab functions and files. Many of these tools are graphical user interfaces. It includes the Scilab desktop and Command Window, a command history, an editor, and browsers for viewing help, the workspace, files, and the search path.

2. The Scilab Mathematical Function Library. This is a vast collection of computational algorithms ranging from elementary functions, like sum, sine, cosine, and complex arithmetic, to more sophisticated functions like matrix inverse, matrix eigenvalues.

3. The Scilab Language. This is a high-level matrix/array language with control flow statements, functions, data structures, input/output, and object-oriented programming features. It allows both "programming in the small" to rapidly create quick programs, and "programming in the large" to create large and complex application programs.

4. Graphics. Scilab has extensive facilities for displaying vectors and matrices as graphs, as well as annotating and printing these graphs. It includes high-level functions for two-dimensional and three-dimensional data visualization, image processing, animation, and presentation graphics. It also includes low-level functions that allow you to fully customize the appearance of graphics as well as to build complete graphical user interfaces on your Scilab applications.

1.3   Scilab Environment

Scilab is easy to start and it has a long time learning curve. It is available in Windows, Apple and Unix environment. Click on the Scilab icon and you will see the **Scilab prompt sign** `-->`. Scilab launches several windows:

- *Command Windows* with prompt sign `-->`. Click in it to activate and type **3+9** and press **Enter** key. The output will be

```
ans  =
   12.
```

- *Current Directory* contains the current directories and files.

- *Workspace* contains the list of available variables with their values and size.

- *Graphics Window* has the figures.

- *Command History* contains list of recent used commands.

- *On-line Help* contains detailed tutorials and manuals that can be searched. Every user should explore the available Scilab documentation on the Help Desk. Scilab Help Desk has many instructive examples and rich programs that can be copied, pasted and modified for your computations.

General Scilab features

1. Scilab is case sensitive, it requires exact match for variable names. For example, if you have a variable name x you can not refer to it as X. At the Command Window type $a = 4$ and **Enter**, type $B = 3$ and **Enter**, type $a + b$ and **Enter**. You will get a message: *!–error 4 Undefined variable: b.* Why this massage and how to fix it?

2. Scilab accepts all kind of data inputs: integer, real, complex, array, characters. No need to specify the type of data. All real numbers are used in double precision.

3. Scilab has *format* function to control the output of numeric values. For example,

    - at the Command Window type $x = \sin(1)$ and **Enter**

    - to change the output to 16 digits, type *format (16); x* and **Enter**

    - to change the output to e-format numbers, type *format('e',10);x* and **Enter**

    - To change to default format (10 digits long), type *format(10)*

    - the maximum number of digits in Scilab format is 25

    - Use the Help Desk to see complete list of available formats.

4. The most common file format is .sce-type such as myfile1.sce which is used for script and function formats.

5. It is advisable that you create a new folder to house and save your files. For Scilab to access your files, you have to change the current directory to your newly created directory (folder). This can be accomplished on the Scilab (Current Directory) icon with the clicks of the mouse.

General Commands

help   lists all available topics for help

who   lists variables n the current directory wit their sizes

clear   removes all variables from the working directory

clc   clears Command Window history, does not affect the variables

clf   clears figures

ls   lists content

date   tells the date

quit   quits Scilab

exit   quits Scilab

1.3.1 *At the Command Window, enter the commands and observe what you see*

    1. help

    2. who

    3. clc

    4. clear

    5. date

1.4   Characters and Operators

Scilab has many types of operators such as arithmetic operators, conditional operators, logical operators and others. It has also predefined characters which are reserved for specific tasks. For complete list and information refer to the Scilab help. Here, we review some of these Scilab notations.

1.4.1   Special Characters

    1. //   **Slashes** Are used to comment a line. Scilab ignores the text following // in a line.

    2. No block comment operator in Scilab, yet!

3. [ ]   **Brackets** are used to form vectors and matrices. For example, the vector X and the matrix Y can be entered as follows

```
-->X=[1 2 4 8] //Enter
 X  =
     1.    2.    4.    8.


-->Y=[1 2 3 4; 2 4 6 8; 1 3 5 9] //Enter
 Y  =
     1.    2.    3.    4.
     2.    4.    6.    8.
     1.    3.    5.    9.
```

Brackets are also used with the output of function statement and on the left side of = in assignments such as *lu, eig* commands. For example, The command $[VE] = spec(A)$ returns the eigenvalues and eigenvectors of the matrix A

```
-->A=[4 -5; 2 -3] \\Enter
 A  =
     4.   - 5.
     2.   - 3.
-->[V E]=spec(A)
 E  =
     2.     0
     0    - 1.
 V  =
     0.9284767     0.7071068
     0.3713907     0.7071068
```

4. ( )   **Parentheses** are used to follow the order of arithmetic operations $3 - (7 - 9)$. They are used in the function statement $f(x, y)$ and to address a subscript in arrays $X(2)$ to call the second entry in the vector X.

5. ,   **Commas** are used for separation between matrix subscripts, function arguments and between statements in lines.

6. ;   **Semicolons** are used after an expression or statement to suppress printing the output or the answer and inside brackets to separate rows of a matrix. For example,

```
-->X=2+4 //Enter
 X  =
     6.
-->Y=2+5; //Enter
--> A=[1 2 3 4 5 6] //Enter
```

```
 A   =
     1.    2.    3.    4.    5.    6.
-->B=[1 2 3; 4 5 6] //Enter
 B   =
     1.    2.    3.
     4.    5.    6.
```

7. **:**   **Colons** are used to create vectors, array subscripting, and for loop iterations. For example,

```
-->X=3:7 //Enter
 X   =
     3.    4.    5.    6.    7.
```

8. **..**   **Continuation** Two or more periods at the end of a line continue the current list and statements on the next line. This allows to enter long statements requiring more than one line.

9. **'**   **Quotation mark** is used to transpose matrices $B = A'$ and quotation marks are used to include character statements such as titles, colors and line marks.

1.4.2 Arithmetic Operators

1. **+**   **Addition** between any numbers. Matrices of same sizes can be added and a number can be added to a matrix. For example,

```
-->2+7 //Enter
 ans   =
     9.
--> A=[1 2 3;2 4 6], B=[1 1 1;2 2 2]
 A   =
     1.    2.    3.
     2.    4.    6.
 B   =
     1.    1.    1.
     2.    2.    2.
->A+B
 ans   =
     2.    3.    4.
     4.    6.    8.
-->10+A
 ans   =
     11.    12.    13.
     12.    14.    16.
```

2. –　　**Subtraction** between any numbers. Matrices of same sizes can be subtracted and a number can be subtracted from a matrix.

3. *　　**Multiplication** of scalars or matrices. For example,

```
--> 3*8 //Enter
 ans  =
     24.
-->A=[1 2;3 4], B=[1 0; 2 5] //Enter
 A  =
     1.    2.
     3.    4.
 B  =
     1.    0.
     2.    5.
-->A*B //Enter
 ans  =
     5.     10.
     11.    20.
```

4. /　　**Slash or matrix right division** for right division $B/A = B * inv(A)$. For example,

```
-->72/18 //Enter
 ans  =
     4.
```

5. \　　**Backslash or matrix left division** for left division $A \backslash B = inv(A) * B$. For example,

```
--> 72\18 //Enter
 ans  =
     0.25
-->A=[1 2;3 4],  b=[2;2], C=A\b, D=inv(A)*b //Enter
 A  =
     1.    2.
     3.    4.
 b  =
     2.
     2.
 C  =
   - 2.
     2.
 D  =
   - 2.
     2.
```

6. ∧   **Power** for exponential operations on scalars and matrices. For example,

```
-->16^(7/4) //Enter
 ans  =
    128.
```

7. .∗   **Matrix multiplication** element-by-element product. $X.∗Y$ is equivalent to the element by element multiplication $X(i,j)∗Y(i,j)$. For example,

```
-->X=[ 1 2 3 4], Y=[5 5 10 10], X.*Y //Enter
 X  =
    1.    2.    3.    4.
 Y  =
    5.    5.    10.    10.
 ans  =
    5.    10.    30.    40.
```

8. ./   **Matrix division** element-by-element quotient. $A./B$ is equivalent to $A(i,j)/B(i,j)$.

9. .∧   **Array power** is the element-by-element raising to power. For example,

```
-->X=[ 1 2 3 4], Z=X.^3 //Enter
 X  =
    1.    2.    3.    4.
 Z  =
    1.    8.    27.    64.
```

10. ′   **Matrix transpose** For example,

```
-->X=[ 1 2 3 4], Y=X' //Enter
 X  =
    1.    2.    3.    4.
 Y  =
    1.
    2.
    3.
    4.
```

1.4.3 Special Values

Variables starting with % represent special built-in constants " Scilab functions".

ans   Most recent answer (variable). If you do not assign an output variable to an expression, Scilab automatically stores the result in ans.

%eps   Floating-point relative accuracy. This is the tolerance Scilab uses in its calculations.

%pi   is $\pi = 3.1415926535897...$

%e   is $e = 2.718181828...$

%i   Imaginary unit. For example,

```
-->(2+3*%i)*(2-3*%i)   //Enter
 ans  =
    13.
```

%inf   Infinity. Calculations like n/0, where n is any nonzero real value, result in inf.

%nan   Not a Number, an invalid numeric value. Expressions like 0/0 and inf/inf result in a %nan , as do arithmetic operations involving a %nan . Also, if n is a complex number with a zero real part, then n/0 returns a value with a %nan real part.

%t   is logical true

%f   is logical false

For example,

```
-->x=10*%pi  //Enter
 x  =
    31.415927
-->tol=2*%eps  //Enter
 tol  =
    4.441D-16
```

1.4.1 *Write the first 24 digits of π and e*

     Solution: *Use the command* format(24); %pi, %e

                                                   □

1.5 Built-in Functions

Scilab has complete set of predefined elementary and specialized mathematical functions that can be located and reviewed in the on-line help documentation. We list the most common functions.

Basic Functions

abs(x)   returns absolute value of x: $|x|$

sign(x)   returns the sign of x, 1 if $x > 0$, -1 if $x < 0$, and 0 if $x = 0$

sqrt(x)   returns the square root of x

exp(x)   returns the exponential function of x: e^x

log(x)   returns the natural logarithm of x: $\ln(x)$

log10(x)   returns the logarithm with base 10 of x: $\log_{10}(x)$

1.6 Saving sessions

To collect all your work in a practice session, you can use *diary* command or script files. As follows

1. diary command: At the prompt sign enter the following commands

   ```
   -->diary('problem1.txt')
    ans  =
         1.
   -->a=2;b=3;
   -->c=2*3
    c  =
         6.
   -->diary(0)
   ```

   The name of your file must be included between quotes. To end your session write diary(0). The file problem1.txt can be found in your current working directory. The default directory is the bin subdirectory of Scilab.

2. Script file: Create a file using SciNotes editor of Scilab. Call your file Problem2.sce

   ```
   // My first script file
   // Name and date
   ```

```
clear
format(6)
x=acos(-1)
format(25)
x
```

Save your script and use the execute icon to run the script Problem2 and perform the calculation.

1.6.1 *For the vector $x = [-4, -2, -1, 0, 1, 9]$, Find the the absolute values and the sign of each element of x. Put all these values in table output.*

At the prompt sign enter the following commands

```
--> x=[-4, -2, -1, 0, 1, 9] //Enter
 x   =
 - 4.   - 2.   - 1.    0.    1.    9.
-->[x;abs(x);sign(x)]
 ans  =
 - 4.   - 2.   - 1.    0.    1.    9.
   4.     2.     1.    0.    1.    9.
 - 1.   - 1.   - 1.    0.    1.    1.
```

1.6.2 *Find the values: e, e^2, $\ln(2)$, $\ln(e^{-2})$.*

At the prompt sign enter the following commands

```
--> exp(1), %e
ans =
    2.7183
--> exp(2), %e^2
ans =
    7.3891
--> log(2)
ans =
    0.6931
--> log(exp(-2))
ans =
    -2
```

Trigonometric Functions

sin(x)   returns the sine in radians of x: **sin(x)**

sind(x)   returns the sine in degrees of x: **sin(x)**

asin(x)   returns the arcsine in radians of x: **arcsin(x)**

cos(x)   returns the cosine in radians of x: **cos(x)**

                                              For a complete list of all

cosd(x)   returns the cosine in degrees of x: **cos(x)**

acos(x)   returns the arccosine in radians of x: **arccos(x)**

tan(x)   returns the tangent in radians of x: **tan(x)**

sinh(x)   returns the sinh in radians of x: **sinh(x)**

trigonometric functions and their inverses refer to Scilab help documentation.

1.6.3 *For the vector* $x = [-\pi \ , 0 \ , \ \pi]$ *find*

1. *$sin(x)$*

2. *$cos(x)$*

At the prompt sign enter the following commands

```
-->format(7)
-->x=[-%pi , 0 , %pi]
 x   =
  - 3.1416    0.    3.1416
-->[x; sin(x); cos(x)]
 ans  =
  - 3.1416    0.    3.1416
  - 1.D-16    0.    1.D-16
  - 1.        1.   - 1.
```

Rounding Functions

round(x)   returns the integer closest to x

fix(x)   returns the integer closest to x in the direction towards zero

             (rounding up for negative numbers, and rounding down for positive numbers)

floor(x)   returns the closest integer below x

ceil(x)   returns the closest integer above x

x-fix(x./y).*y   returns the remainder of the integer division x/y

1.6.4 *Use Scilab to make a table containing the vector*

$$x = \begin{bmatrix} -2.4 & -1.7 & -.5 & -.2 & 0.0 & .6 & 1.49 & 1.9 \end{bmatrix}$$

and the value of the functions round(x), fix(x), ceil(x), floor(x)

At the prompt sign enter the following commands

```
-->x=[-2.4, -1.7,  -.2, 0, .6,  1.9];
-->[x;round(x);fix(x);ceil(x);floor(x)]
 ans  =
  - 2.4  - 1.7  - 0.2    0.    0.6    1.9
  - 2.   - 2.     0.     0.    1.     2.
  - 2.   - 1.     0.     0.    0.     1.
  - 2.   - 1.     0.     0.    1.     2.
  - 3.   - 2.   - 1.     0.    0.     1.
```

Discrete Functions

1. x-fix(x./y).*y returns the remainder of the integer division x/y

2. lcm((x,y)) returns the least common multiple of positive integers x and y

3. factor(x) returns the prime factors of x

4. (n,d)=rat(x) returns x as fraction

5. factorial(x) returns the factorial of $x!$

6. primes(x) returns all the prime numbers less than x

1.6.5 *Use Scilab to answer the following questions:*

1. *Factor* **182672**

2. *is* $2^{2^5} + 1$ *prime?*

3. *Find* **20!**

4. *Approximate* $\sqrt{2}$ *as a rational number*

    Solution: *Use the following Scilab commands:*

1. *factor*(**182672**) *and show that* $182672 = (2^4)(7^2)(233)$

2. *factor*($2^{2^5} + 1$) *results in an error. Scilab can not find the factorization, but Euler was able to show that* $2^{32} + 1 = (641)(6700417)$. *Use Scilab to show the equality!*

3. *factorial(20)=2432902008176640000*

4. *[n, d]=rat (sqrt(2))= 1393/985*

                                                                     □

Data Analysis Functions

max(x)	returns the largest value in each column of x
min(x)	returns the smallest value in each column of x
mean(x)	returns the average value in each column of x
median(x)	returns the median value of each column of x
sum(x)	returns the sum value of each column of x
product(x)	returns the product value of elements of each column of x
sort(x)	returns the sorted values in ascending (increasing) order of each colu
sort(x,'descend')	returns the sorted values in descending order of each column of x

1.7 Homework: Basics

Use Scilab to answer the following questions

1.7.1 *Compute the following values*

1. $sin(\pi/6)$

2. e^2

3. arccos(0.5)

4. For $t = 36$ *degree, find* tan(t)

1.7.2 *Compute the following values*

1. *Round the numbers to the nearest integer:* **2.3, 2.5, 2.7**

2. *The remainder of* **48/11**

3. *the prime factorization of* **732**

4. *Rationalize the numbers* **0.125** *and* π

5. *compute* **10!**

1.7.3 *Compute the following:*

1. $6\dfrac{5}{17}$

2. $-\dfrac{3}{10} + 3^{-5}$

3. $-4.023^{4.023}$

4. *Rationalize* cos($\pi/5$)

1.7.4 *Approximate the following numbers to 20 digits:*

1. $\sqrt{2}$

2. $\sqrt[3]{2}$

1.7.5 *Find the number of digits of the periodic decimal notation of the following rational numbers*

1. $\dfrac{1}{3}$

2. $\dfrac{1}{7}$

3. $\dfrac{1}{13}$

1.7.6 *Given that* $a = 2, \quad b = -3, \quad c = 5$, *compute the expressions*

1. $a - b \cdot c$

2. $c + \dfrac{c - a \cdot b}{a - b - c}$

3. $a - \dfrac{b^3 - a \cdot c}{a \cdot c - b}$

1.7.7 *Evaluate the expressions*

1. 5^{3^2}

2. $(5^3)^2$

3. $5^{(3^2)}$

1.7.8 *Evaluate the expressions*

1. $\sqrt{2}, \pi, e$

2. $\sin(\pi/3)$

3. $\sqrt{3}/2$

4. $\sin^2(\pi/3) + \cos^2(\pi/3)$

5. $\cos 45^0 - \dfrac{\sqrt{2}}{2}$

6. $\dfrac{2}{\pi} \cdot \arctan(\tan(\dfrac{\pi}{4}))$

2 | Matrices

In this chapter we provide a short introduction to operations on vectors and matrices and their use in solving linear systems of equations.

1 Definition An $m \times n$ matrix is a two dimensional array of numbers. The $m \times n$ matrix

$$A = \begin{bmatrix} a_{11} & a_{12} & a_{13} & \cdots & a_{1n} \\ a_{21} & a_{22} & a_{23} & \cdots & a_{2n} \\ a_{31} & a_{32} & a_{33} & \cdots & a_{3n} \\ \vdots & \vdots & \vdots & & \vdots \\ a_{m1} & a_{m2} & a_{m3} & \cdots & a_{mn} \end{bmatrix}$$

The matrix A has m rows and n columns. Scilab has hypermatrix type to manipulate multidimensional matrices. In this chapter, we will introduce the main functions and operations of generating matrices, extracting data from arrays, using special matrices, and applications to solve problem in linear algebra.

2.1 Generating Matrices

The 2×3 matrix $A = \begin{bmatrix} 2 & 1 & 2 \\ 3 & 2 & 3 \end{bmatrix}$ can be defined by typing the numbers separated by spaces or commas and the rows are separated by semicolons. All numbers are enclosed in **square brackets**. At the prompt sign enter the following commands

```
--> A=[2 1 2;3 2 3] //enter
 A   =
    2.    1.    2.
    3.    2.    3.
```

or by entering

```
--> A=[2,1,2;3,2,3]
```

At the prompt sign enter the following commands

```
-->X=[1 2 3 4 5], Y=[1;2;3;4]
 X  =
    1.    2.    3.    4.    5.
 Y  =
    1.
    2.
    3.
    4.
```

2.1.1 *Enter the matrix A by taking advantage of the pattern in the matrix*

$$A = \begin{bmatrix} 1/2 & 1/3 & 0 & 0 \\ 1/3 & 1/2 & 1/3 & 0 \\ 0 & 1/3 & 1/2 & 1/3 \\ 0 & 0 & 1/3 & 1/2 \end{bmatrix}$$

Type at the prompt sign

```
-->x=1/2;y=1/3;

--> A=[x y 0 0;y x y 0; 0 y x y;0 0 y x]
 A  =
    0.5        0.3333     0.        0.
    0.3333     0.5        0.3333    0.
    0.         0.3333     0.5       0.3333
    0.         0.         0.3333    0.5
```

2.1.2 *Enter the Vandermonde matrix B by taking advantage of its pattern:*

$$B = \begin{bmatrix} 1 & 1 & 1 & 1 \\ x & y & z & w \\ x^2 & y^2 & z^2 & w^2 \\ x^3 & y^3 & z^3 & w^3 \end{bmatrix}$$

Where $x = 2, y = 3, z = -2, w = -3$

Solution: *Construct numerical row R as follows*

```
-->x=2; y=3; z=-2; w=-3;
-->R=[x y z w];
-->B=[R.^0; R; R.^2; R.^3] // Note the dot power:element by element
 B  =
    1.    1.    1.    1.
    2.    3.  - 2.  - 3.
    4.    9.    4.    9.
    8.   27.  - 8.  - 27.
```

□

2.1.1 Generating vectors

The colon operator : and the *linspace* functions are the most common tools to generate new vectors and matrices. For example,

V1=a:b	returns a sequence of numbers starting with *a* and ending with *b* in steps of one.
V2=a:s:b	returns a sequence of numbers starting with *a*m and ending with *b* in steps of *s*
V3=linspace(a,b)	returns a vector with **100** equally spaced values between *a* and *b*
V4=linspace(a,b,n)	returns a vector with *n* equally spaced values between *a* and *b*

For example, to generate a vector *Z* with **11** uniform points between **0** and **1**. Enter

```
-->Z=linspace(0,1,11)
 Z  =
    0.    0.1    0.2    0.3    0.4    0.5    0.6    0.7    0.8    0.9    1.
```

At the prompt sign enter the following commands

```
-->V1=-6:3:9,  V2=5:12
 V1  =
  - 6.  - 3.    0.    3.    6.    9.
 V2  =
    5.    6.    7.    8.    9.   10.   11.   12.
```

2.1.3 *Create the following matrices using Scilab*

$$A = \begin{bmatrix} 11 & 15 & -3 & 2 \end{bmatrix} \qquad B = \begin{bmatrix} 1 & 2 & 3 \\ -2 & 3 & 4 \\ -3 & -4 & 5 \end{bmatrix} \qquad C = \begin{bmatrix} -1 \\ 13 \\ -2 \end{bmatrix}$$

2.1.4 *Construct a matrix that will hold the triples of data* $(1, x, -x)$ *where* $x = [0, 1, 2, 3, 4, 5]$.

```
-->x=0:5;
-->A=[1+0*x ; x ; -x]
 A   =
    1.    1.    1.    1.    1.    1.
    0.    1.    2.    3.    4.    5.
    0.  - 1.  - 2.  - 3.  - 4.  - 5.
```

2.1.5 *Use Scilab to create*

1. S1=4:13, S2=9:-2:0

2. S3=0:pi/10:pi

3. V1=linspace(1,2,50)

2.1.6 *Use Scilab to answer*

1. *Generate* **10** *equally spaced points between* **–1** *and* **1** *in a vector format.*

2. *Generate a vector of points between* **0** *and* **18** *with step size* **3** *and using* **:** *operator.*

3. *Generate a vector of points between* **6** *and* **–9** *with step size* **–3** *and using* **:** *operator.*

2.1.7 *Use Scilab to generate odd and even numbers less than 30 in two columns matrix.*

```
--> x=1:2:30; y=2:2:30;
--> B=[x' y']
```

2.1.8 *Use Scilab to generate*

1. *Odd numbers between* **80** *and* **100**.

2. *The numbers* **30, 45, 60, ⋯, 150**

2.1.9   *1. What are the first and last output generated by* linspace(0,π) *and how many outputs in all?*

2. *What is the* linspace *command generating the vector* **0.2, 0.3, 0.4, 0.5, 0.6, 0.7, 0.8** *?*

2.1.2 Size of Variables

We can keep track of the dimensions of all variables and arrays by using the commands

    size(A)   returns the number of rows and columns of *A*

    length(x)   returns the length of a vector *x*

2.1.10 *Construct the matrices*

$$B = \begin{bmatrix} 1 & 2 & 3 \\ \\ -2 & 3 & 4 \end{bmatrix} \qquad C = \begin{bmatrix} -1 & 13 & -2 & 9 \end{bmatrix}$$

At the prompt sign enter

```
>> size(B)
>> size(C)
>> length(C)
```

2.1.3 Generating submatrices

For a given matrix A, using the operator :, we define

    A(i,j)   returns the element a_{ij}

    A(:,j)   returns the jth column of *A*

    A(i,:)   returns the ith row of *A*

    A(:,j:k)   returns the columns j,j+1, ..., k of submatrix of *A*

    A(:)   returns *A* as one column

2.1.11 *Define the matrix* $A = \begin{bmatrix} 1 & -2 & 3 \\ -4 & 5 & -6 \\ 7 & -8 & 9 \end{bmatrix}$

1. *Extract the second column of A. Use* `A(:,2)`

2. *Extract the third row of A*

3. *Extract The matrix* $B^{2\times2}$ *from the upper right part of A. Use* `B= A(1:2,2:3)`

4. *Reconfigure A so that all elements of A are put in one vector. Use* `A(:)`

2.1.12 *Enter the matrix* $X = \begin{bmatrix} -2 & 1 & 4 & 1 \\ 4 & 0 & 2 & -5 \\ 17 & 3 & -1 & 8 \end{bmatrix}$

1. *Extract the first row and store it in* v

2. *Extract the entry* **17** *and store it in* c

3. *Extract The matrix* $B^{2\times2}$ *from the lower right part of X*

Generating new matrices

Matrices of ones, zeros are generated as follows:

ones (m,n)   returns an $m \times n$ matrix of ones

zeros (m,n)   returns an $m \times n$ matrix of zeros

zeros (size(A))   returns a matrix of zeros of size A

eye (m,n)   returns an $m \times n$ identity matrix

eye (size(A))   returns identity matrix of size A

2.1.13 *Generate the matrices*

1. M1=ones(3,4)

2. M2=eye(3,3)

3. M3=zeros(2,5)

4. M4=ones(size(M3))

2.2 Matrix Operations

Let us define a vector $X = [1,2,3,4]$ and $Y = [-1,0,-1,0,5]$. At the prompt sign enter the following commands and explain the output

```
--> X+X
--> 5*X
--> Y-7*Y
--> size(X)
--> size(Y)
--> X+Y
--> X*X
--> X.*X % Do not forget the dot!
--> X^3
--> X.^3
```

Addition of Matrices

In the following problems we are going to perform basic operations of matrix algebra. The addition and subtraction of matrices are well defined provided they have the same size.

2.2.1 *Given that* $A = \begin{bmatrix} 3 & -2 \\ 5 & -4 \end{bmatrix}$ *and* $B = \begin{bmatrix} 3 & 4 \\ 2 & 5 \end{bmatrix}$

Find:

1. A+B

2. A-B

3. A+10

Multiplication of Matrices

The multiplication of matrices $C = AB$ is defined provided the number of columns of $A^{m \times n}$ is the same as the number of rows of $B^{n \times p}$. The operator $*$ is used in Scilab for matrix multiplication.

2.2.2 *Given that* $A = \begin{bmatrix} 3 & -2 \\ 5 & -4 \end{bmatrix}$, $B = \begin{bmatrix} 3 & 4 \\ 2 & 5 \end{bmatrix}$, $u = [2 \quad ,4 \quad ,6]$ *and* $v = \begin{bmatrix} 10 \\ -1 \\ 1 \end{bmatrix}$

Compute, if possible:

1. AB

2. BA

3. uv

4. vu

Matrix Powers

Raising a square matrix A to power n is accomplished by successive multiplication. For example, $A^3 = AAA$. In Scilab, we use the power command: A^2, A^3, A^4, ...

2.2.3 *Given that* $A = \begin{bmatrix} 1 & 1 \\ 0 & 1 \end{bmatrix}$, $B = \begin{bmatrix} 2 & -1 \\ 3 & -2 \end{bmatrix}$

Find:

1. A^2, A^3, A^{10} *and* A^{100}. *Make a generalization about* A^n *for any natural number* n.

2. B^2, B^3, B^4 . *Make a generalization about* B^n *as* n *increases.*

Row Operations

Scilab has a default function to compute the reduced row echelon for (RREF). Scilab has a built-in function

```
rref(A)
```

to compute the RREF form of any matrix.

2.2.4 *Determine the reduced row echelon form of A:*

1. $A = \begin{bmatrix} 1 & 3 & 1 \\ -3 & -6 & 1 \\ 1 & 3 & 0 \end{bmatrix}$, $B = \begin{bmatrix} 1 & 2 & 3 \\ 4 & 6 & 0 \\ 2 & 3 & 0 \end{bmatrix}$, $C = \begin{bmatrix} 1 & 3 & 1 & 5 \\ -3 & -6 & 1 & 0 \\ 1 & 3 & 0 & 2 \end{bmatrix}$

2. $A = \begin{bmatrix} 3 & 1 & -2 & 14 \\ 3 & 1 & 1 & 15 \\ 2 & 0 & -2 & 11 \end{bmatrix}$

3. $A = \begin{bmatrix} -3 & 1 & -2 \\ 2 & 4 & -2 \\ 2 & 0 & 3 \\ 1 & 4 & 2 \end{bmatrix}$

Solution:

```
-->A=[1 3 1;-3 -6 1;1 3 0]; RA=rref(A)
 RA  =
    1.    0.    0.
    0.    1.    0.
    0.    0.    1.
-->B=[1 2 3; 4 6 0; 2 3 0]; RB=rref(B)
 RB  =
    1.    0.   - 9.
    0.    1.    6.
    0.    0.    0.
-->C=[1 3 1 5;-3 -6 1 0;1 3 0 2]; RC=rref(C)
 RC  =
    1.    0.    0.   - 1.
    0.    1.    0.    1.
    0.    0.    1.    3.
```

□

Vector Products

Given the vectors $a = \begin{bmatrix} a_1 & a_2 & a_3 \end{bmatrix}$ and $b = \begin{bmatrix} b_1 & b_2 & b_3 \end{bmatrix}$.

The dot product is defined by the scalar $a \cdot b = a_1 b_1 + a_2 b_2 + a_3 b_3$ and
the cross product is the vector given by $a \times b = (a_2 b_3 - a_3 b_2 \quad , a_3 b_1 - a_1 b_3 \quad , a_1 b_2 - a_2 b_1)$

2.2.5 *Given that* $u = [2, \quad 4, \quad 6]$ *and* $v = \begin{bmatrix} 10 \\ -1 \\ 1 \end{bmatrix}$

1. *Find the dot product of* u *and* v.

   Solution:

   ```
   --> u=[2 4 6]; v=[10;-1;1];
   --> dotuv=u*v
   dotuv =
       22
   ```

   □

2.2.6 *Find the lengths and the angle between the vector* $a = [3, \quad 7, \quad 1]$ *and* $b = [6, \quad -3, \quad -3]$ *. Use the cosine formula*

$$\cos(\theta) = \frac{a \cdot b}{\sqrt{|a|}\sqrt{|b|}}$$

where $a \cdot b$ *is the inner product and* $|a|, |b|$ *are the lengths of vectors* a *and* b.

Solution:

```
-->a=[3 7 1]; b=[6 -3 -3];
-->length_a=sqrt(a*a') // Note the transpose
 length_a  =
    7.6811457
-->length_b=sqrt(b*b') // Note the transpose
 length_b  =
    7.3484692
-->ab=a*b';
-->cos_theta=ab/(length_a*length_b)
 cos_theta  =
  - 0.1062988
```

```
-->theta=acos(cos_theta)
 theta  =
    1.6772963
-->theta_deg=theta/(%pi)*180
 theta_deg  =
    96.102001
```

$\square$

Division of Matrices

The forward slash and backslash operators are used to solve linear equations. The solution of the system $A*X = b$ is $X = A\backslash b$ (left division) and the solution of $Y*A = b$ is $Y = b/A$ (right division).

2.2.7 *Solve the system of equations*

$$x + 3y = 1$$

$$2x - 4y = 3$$

Solution: *We write the system of equations in the form* $AX = b$ *where*

```
-->A=[1 3; 2 -4]; b=[1; 3];
-->X=A\b
 X  =
     1.3
   - 0.1
```

$\square$

2.2.8 *Given that* $A = \begin{bmatrix} 3 & -2 \\ 5 & -4 \end{bmatrix}$ *and* $b = \begin{bmatrix} 10 \\ -1 \end{bmatrix}$.

Find the solution of the system $AX = b$. *Using left division* $X = A\backslash b$ *and check your solution by multiplying* $A * X$.

Transposition

The transposition of matrix $A^{m \times n}$ is the matrix $B^{n \times m}$ where $b_{ij} = a_{ji}$. In Scilab, the **apostrophe** $'$ is used for the transpose operation, so the matrix B defined by B=A$'$ is the transpose of A.

2.2.9 *Given that* $X = \begin{bmatrix} 2 & -2 \\ 5 & 3 \end{bmatrix}$ *and* $Y = \begin{bmatrix} 10 & 3 \\ -1 & 0 \\ 4 & 9 \end{bmatrix}$.

Find the transpositions of X and Y.

Elementwise Arithmetic Operations

Arithmetic operations on element by element are done on matrices of equal sizes. The element-by-element operations are + , - , .* , .^ , .\ , ./ . The dot is required before the multiplication, division and power.

2.2.10 *For the matrix A and the array X given by*

```
--> A=[7 8 1; 1 -1 2; 10 5 0]
A =
     7     8     1
     1    -1     2
    10     5     0
--> X=[-1 0 1 2 3 5]
X =
    -1     0     1     2     3     5
```

Compute and compare

1. SA=A + A , A2=2.*A

2. Adot=A.*A, Ap=A.^2 , Ap2=A^2, Am=A*A

3. Y1= 3*X, Y2=X.^2, Y3=X.^3,

4. *What happens to* Y4= X^4? *Explain.*

Solution:

```
--> Adot=A.*A
Adot =
     49    64     1
      1     1     4
    100    25     0
--> Ap=A.^2
Ap =
     49    64     1
```

```
         1      1      4
       100     25      0
--> Ap2=A^2
Ap2 =
        67     53     23
        26     19     -1
        75     75     20
--> Am=A*A
Am =
        67     53     23
        26     19     -1
        75     75     20
```

We conclude that The first two operations are element by element multiplications while the last two operations are the standard matrix multiplications and power operation.

□

2.2.11 *Given that* $X = \begin{bmatrix} 2 & -2 \\ 2 & 3 \end{bmatrix}$ *and* $Y = \begin{bmatrix} 10 & 3 \\ -1 & 0 \\ 4 & 9 \end{bmatrix}$.

1. Compare the products: X1=X * X *and* X2=X .* X

2. Compute Y .* Y.

3. What happens to the product Y * Y? *Explain.*

Construction of Matrices

Random matrices can be generated by the rand function which produces uniformly distributed random number between **0** and **1** or by: the rand('normal') function which produces normally distributed random number with a mean **0** and a variance **1**. Also, rand('uniform') is the same as the default.

rand	returns uniformly distributed random number between 0 and 1
rand(n,m,'uniform')	returns an $n \times m$ matrix with entries uniformly distributed randon numbers between 0 and 1
rand('normal')	returns normally distributed random number with a mean 0 and variance 1
randn(n,m,'normal')	returns an $n \times m$ matrix with entries normally distributed randon numbers

2.2.12 *At the prompt sign enter the following commands:*

1. rand('uniform'), a=rand(), b=rand(1,4), c=rand(10,1), *and* d=rand(4,2)

2. rand('normal'),x=rand(), y=rand(4,1), *and* z=rand(3,5)

3. t=rand(2250,1,'uniform'); histplot(10,t). *What is the shape of the histogram?*

4. s=rand(2250,1,'normal'); histplot(15,s). *What is the shape of the histogram?*

The rand makes probabilistic simulation of various probability distributions very simple. One of the simple techniques is the inverse transformation method. The exponential distribution is given by $-\log(1-x)$, where x is a uniform distribution.

2.2.13 *Using Scilab command answer the following*

1. *Simulate and graph a uniform random distribution of 3000 values between 5 and 6.*

2. *Simulate and graph an exponential random distribution of 3000 values.*

3. *Simulate and graph three normal random distributions of 3000 values.*

Solution: *At the prompt sign, enter:*

```
--> x=rand(3000,1,'uniform');histplot(20,x+5) % 20 is the number of bins
--> u=-log(1-x);histplot(20,u)
--> y=rand(3000,1,'normal');histplot(20,y)
```

The graphs of these matrices demonstrate the type of distributions. □

New Matrices from Given Matrices

For a given matrix $A^{m \times n}$, and X is a vector with n components, the commands diag, triu, tril create new matrices as in the table

diag(A)   returns a column vector of the main diagonal of A

diag(X)   returns a square matrix $n \times n$ with X as its main diagonal and zero elsewhere.

diag(A,k)   returns a column vector of the k diagonal of A where $k = 0$ is the main diagonal and $k > 0$ from over the main and $k < 0$ from below the main.

diag(X,k)   returns $(n + abs(k)) \times (n + abs(k))$ matrix with vector X on the kth diagonal.

triu(A)   returns an upper triangular matrix of A size.

tril(A)   returns a lower triangular matrix of A size.

2.2.14 *Suppose $A = \begin{bmatrix} 8 & 5 & 7 \\ -3 & -6 & 4 \\ -9 & 2 & 1 \end{bmatrix}$*

Find the upper and lower triangular matrices of A.

Solution: *Uppertriangular = triu (A) and Lowertriangular = tril(A, -1) return:*

```
-->A=[8, 5, 7;-3, -6, 4; -9, 2, 1]
 A   =
     8.      5.      7.
  - 3.    - 6.      4.
  - 9.      2.      1.
-->Uppertriangular = triu(A)
 Uppertriangular   =
     8.      5.      7.
     0.    - 6.      4.
     0.      0.      1.
-->Lowertriangular = tril(A, -1)
 Lowertriangular   =
```

```
    0.    0.    0.
  - 3.    0.    0.
  - 9.    2.    0.
```

☐

2.2.15 *Define* A=rand(4,5,'normal') *and* X=[1,−2,3,−4]. *Find*

1. A1=diag(A),A2=diag(diag(A))

2. X1=diag(X), X2=diag(X')

3. A3=diag(A),A4=diag(A,0), A5=diag(A,1), A6=diag(A,2),A7=diag(A,-1)

4. ATU=triu(A), ATL=tril(A, -1)

5. *Print out the matrix*
   D=4*eye(5)+diag(-1*ones(1,3),2)+diag(-1*ones(1,3),-2)

2.3 Systems of Linear Equations

Basic Functions of matrices

det(A)   returns the determinant of a square matrix **A**

rank(A)   returns the rank of **A** that is the number of linearly independent columns and rows

inv(A)   returns the inverse of a square matrix **A**

trace (A)   returns the determinant of a square matrix **A**

2.3.1 *For the matrix* $A = \begin{bmatrix} 0 & 1 & 1 & 1 \\ 1 & 0 & 1 & 1 \\ 1 & 1 & 0 & 1 \\ 1 & 1 & 1 & 0 \end{bmatrix}$,

Compute

1. D1=det(A) , R1=rank(A) , *and* T1=trace (A)

2. B=inv(A) . *Check the matrix.*

Solving linear systems

To solve the linear system of equations $Ax = b$, where A is the coefficient matrix, b is a given vector, the unknown vector solution x is equal to $x = A^{-1}b$ if the inverse matrix A^{-1} exists. We also can compute the solution using x=A\b

2.3.2 *Solve the matrix equation* $A = \begin{bmatrix} 2 & 2 & -1 & 1 \\ 4 & 3 & -1 & 2 \\ 8 & 5 & -3 & 4 \\ 3 & 3 & -2 & 2 \end{bmatrix} \begin{bmatrix} x \\ y \\ z \\ w \end{bmatrix} = \begin{bmatrix} 4 \\ 6 \\ 12 \\ 6 \end{bmatrix}$

Solution:

```
--> A=[2 2 -1 1; 4 3 -1 2; 8 5 -3 4; 3 3 -2 2]
A =
      2      2     -1      1
      4      3     -1      2
      8      5     -3      4
      3      3     -2      2
--> b=[4;6;12;6];
--> X=inv(A)*b
X =
      1
      1
     -1
     -1
--> A*X // Check the solution AX=b
ans =
      4
      6
     12
      6
--> X=A\b // Using the division
X =
      1.0000
      1.0000
     -1.0000
     -1.0000
```

□

Gauss-Jordan Elimination

For the general matrix equation $Ax = b$, where A can be a rectangular matrix, we combine the right side with the matrix A to get the **augmented matrix** and we calculate the reduced row echelon form to find the solution.

2.3.3 *Solve the system*

$$-2x + y + 2z = 4$$

$$x - 4y - 2z = -6$$

$$-x + 2y - 2z = 2$$

using Gauss-Jordan elimination.

Solution: *Write the augmented matrix and use rref function*

```
--> A=[-2 1 2 4; 1 -4 -2 -6; -1 2 -2 2], AR=rref(A)
A =
    -2     1     2     4
     1    -4    -2    -6
    -1     2    -2     2
AR =
    1.0000         0         0    -1.0000
         0    1.0000         0     1.0000
         0         0    1.0000     0.5000
```

The solution is the vector $(x, y, z) = (-1, 1, 0.5)$

$\square$

2.3.4 *Given the matrix* $A = \begin{bmatrix} 2 & 2 & -1 & 1 \\ 4 & 3 & -1 & 2 \\ 8 & 5 & -3 & 4 \\ 3 & 3 & -2 & 2 \end{bmatrix}$, *and the vector* $b = [4, 6, 12, 6]'$.

Find the solution of $AX = b$.

Eigenvalues and Eigenvectors

For a square matrix the solution of $Ax = \lambda x$ is eigenvalue-eigenvector problem.

spec (A)   returns the eigenvalues of A as a vector

(V, D)=spec (A)   returns A matrix V of eigenvectors and a matrix D of eigenvalues of A

2.3.5 *Find the eigenvalues and eigenvectors of the matrix A:*

$A = \begin{bmatrix} 1 & -3 & 4 \\ 4 & -7 & 8 \\ 6 & -7 & 7 \end{bmatrix}$

Solution:

```
--> A=[1 -3 4;4 -7 8; 6 -7 7]
A =
      1     -3      4
      4     -7      8
      6     -7      7
--> [V D]=spec(A)
V =
     0.3333    -0.4082    -0.4082
     0.6667    -0.8165    -0.8165
     0.6667    -0.4082    -0.4082
D =
     3.0000         0         0
          0   -1.0000         0
          0         0   -1.0000
```

□

2.3.6 *Solve the system*

$$-2x + y + z = -1$$

$$3x + y + 2z = 1$$

$$-5x + 2x - z = 3$$

Verify that the obtained answer satisfies the system.

Solution:

```
-->A=[-2 1 1;3 1 2;-5 2 -1];b=[-1;1;3];
-->x=A\b
  x  =
     0.7857
     2.5
   - 1.9286
-->A*x
  ans  =
   - 1.
     1.
     3.
```

□

2.4 Homework: Matrices

Use Scilab to answer the following:

2.4.1 *1. Generate* **20** *equally spaced points between* **0** *and* π *in a vector format.*

2. Generate a vector of points between **−12** *and* **12** *with step size* **2** *and using* **:** *operator.*

2.4.2 *Find the length of the vector* $V = (2 \quad -3 \quad 4 \quad -5)$.

2.4.3 *Find the length of the vector* $V = (-2 \quad 1+i \quad -3i \quad 3)$.

2.4.4 *The components of a vector* V *are* $-3, 2, 1-i, \pi$. *Enter this vector in row and column format.*

2.4.5 *Create a* 6×6 *matrix* A *with twos on the diagonal and zeroes everywhere else.*

2.4.6 *Create a* 7×7 *matrix* B *with zeroes on the diagonal and threes everywhere else.*

2.4.7 *Compute the array product* $A.*B$ *and the matrix product* AB *of the matrices*

$$A = \begin{bmatrix} 3 & -2 & 0 \\ 5 & -4 & 1 \\ 0 & 1 & -1 \end{bmatrix} \quad and \quad B = \begin{bmatrix} 0 & 3 & 4 \\ 2 & -5 & 0 \\ -1 & 0 & 1 \end{bmatrix}$$

2.4.8 *Find the eigenvalues and eigenvectors of the matrices* A *and* B:

$$A = \begin{bmatrix} 3 & -1 & 0 & 0 \\ 1 & 1 & 0 & 0 \\ 3 & 0 & 5 & -3 \\ 4 & -1 & 3 & -1 \end{bmatrix} \quad and \quad B = \begin{bmatrix} 1 & 2 & 3 \\ 4 & 5 & 6 \\ 7 & 8 & 9 \end{bmatrix}$$

2.4.9 *Solve the linear system of equations*

$$x + y - z = 1$$

$$2x - y + z = 2$$

$$-4y + 3z = 12$$

using three different methods

1. *Matrix division method*

2. *Inverse matrix method*

3. *Augmented matrix (Reduced row echelon form) method*

2.4.10 *Solve the matrix equation* $A = \begin{bmatrix} 1 & 4 & -3 & 4 \\ -1 & 1 & -1 & 4 \\ -2 & -1 & -1 & 4 \\ -2 & 0 & -1 & 2 \end{bmatrix} \begin{bmatrix} x \\ y \\ z \\ w \end{bmatrix} = \begin{bmatrix} 2 \\ 12 \\ -6 \\ -12 \end{bmatrix}$

|3| Programming

3.1 Script-files

There are three ways to interact with Scilab

1. Simply by typing directly to Scilab window the input parameters, commands and required output parameters. This way is the most common and easy to accomplish for short tasks.

2. Scripts (sce-files): There is a Scilab editor to create files and save all your work for future use and repetitive tasks. They can use any variable in the workspace when the script is run , and the results of the script are stored in the workspace for use.

3. functions: These are sce-files also, they are created by users to enhance Scilab for their projects and usually require input and output variables. They can take dynamic inputs, but all variables are local to the function and they are not saved in the workspace.

Script file

Let us write a script file to draw a unit disc in red color. Save the script as unitdisc.sce and run it.

```
// date name
// unitcircle
t=linspace(0,2*%pi,200); //create a vector t
x=sin(t); // x-coordinate
y=cos(t); //y-coordinate
plot(x,y,'g')
halt() // This command pauses until you hit any key
x=sin(2*t); // x-coordinate
y=cos(5*t); //y-coordinate
plot(x,y,'r')
title (' Unit Circle')
```

43

Function file

The function file must start with a function definition line, which includes the name, the input and output variables. If you do not include this line, the file is simply a script file and not a function file. The syntax is:

```
function [outputs, variables ] = function_name( inputs, variables)
\\Statements
endfunction
```

where the *function_name* **must be the same as the file name.**

3.1.1 *Construct a cubing function* $y = x^3$. *Check the function at* $x = -2$ *and* $x = 5$.

```
// Simple function with one input and one output
// -----------------------------------------------------
function y = f(x) ; y = x^3; endfunction // Run this script
-->f(-2) // Enter
 ans  =
  - 8.
-->f(5)
 ans  =
    125.
```

3.1.2 *Construct a cubic function* $y = x^3$ *and its derivative at any value.*

```
// Simple function with one input and two outputs
// The outputs are the values of the cubic function and its derivative at a point
// ---------------
function [y, dy] = f(x); // Notice the bracket for vector output
 y = x^3; dy = 3*x ^2; endfunction // Run this script
-->[y, dy]=f(2)  // Enter
 dy  =
    12.
 y  =
    8.
```

In the following we will create a function to paint a disc with any center, radius and color. Such file has advantage that it can be used repeatedly to create discs. We will call this function discplot and the saved file must be called discplot.sce

```
// discplot is a function to paint a circle with given
// center (h,k) and radius r, and optional input such as
// colors: c= 1 black; 2 blue; 3 green; 4 cyan; 5r red, and so on
// -------------------------------------------------------
function discplot(h,k,r,c)
t=linspace(0,2*%pi,200);
```

```
x=h+r*sin(t);
y=k+r*cos(t);
//plot(x,y)
plot2d(0,0,-1,'010',' ',[-10,-10,10,10])//last vector specifies the domain
xset('color',c)
xfpoly(x,y)
endfunction
```

3.1.3 *Execute the file directly from the editor icon, after that, at the command window type the following*

```
-->discplot(3,3,2,5)
-->discplot(-3,-3,2,5)
-->discplot(-3,3,2,2)
-->discplot(3,-3,2,2)
```

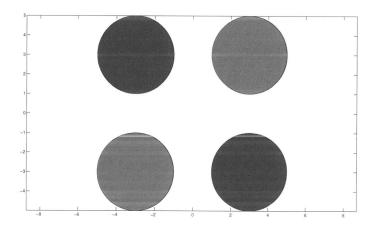

Figure 3.1: Four discs

3.1.4 *Run the script file multidiscs.sce to produce the circular design of figure 3.2*

```
//multidiscs - A script to draw a circular design
//   ----------------------------------------------------
// inner discs
discplot(0, 0, 4, 2)
discplot(0, 0, 3, 4)
discplot(0, 0, 2, 1)
discplot(0, 0, 1, 5)
// outer discs
discplot(5, 0, 1, 5) ,discplot(5, 0, .8, 1) //left
```

```
discplot(5, 0, .6, 4),discplot(5, 0, .4, 2)
discplot(0, 5, 1, 5) ,discplot(0, 5, .8, 1) //top
discplot(0, 5, .6, 4),discplot(0, 5, .4, 2)
discplot(0, -5, 1, 5) ,discplot(0, -5, .8, 1) //bottom
discplot(0, -5, .6, 4),discplot(0, -5, .4, 2)
discplot(-5, 0, 1, 5) ,discplot(-5, 0, .8, 1) //right
discplot(-5, 0, .6, 4),discplot(-5, 0, .4, 2)
```

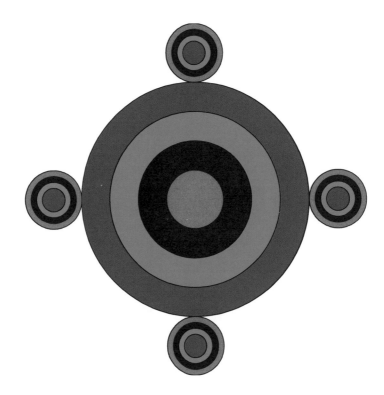

Figure 3.2: Multidiscs

3.1.5 *Look at figure 3.3 and compare the central two discs on left and right side. Which disc is larger: Central Left or Central Right?. This is a classic visual illusion. Write a script file by calling the function discplot.sce to produce the figure 3.3.*

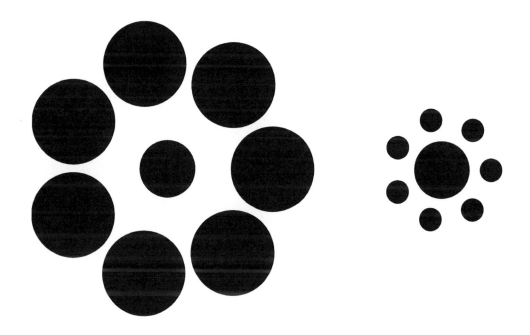

Figure 3.3: Circular illusion

3.2   Scilab Time functions

Scilab has functions to record time and duration of calculations. These are

1. timer() returns the total CPU time (in seconds) used by Scilab from the time it was started.

2. clock returns a 6-element date vector containing the current date and time in decimal format: [year month day hour minute seconds]

3. etime(t2, t1) returns the time in seconds between different time points.

4. tic and toc Two functions work together to measure elapsed time

5. date current date

3.3 Basic Scilab Programming

Scilab scripting has The main control functions are well defined in Scilab scripting which allows for writing efficient codes and speedy calculations. **The conditional statements** are

1. Greater: $A > B$

2. Smaller: $A < B$

3. Equal: $A == B$

4. And: $A \& B$

5. Or: $A \mid B$

6. Not-equal: $A \sim= B$

If statement

The *if* statement is to execute statements if a certain condition is satisfied. We also, have *ifelse* and or *else*. Each *if* must be matched with an *end*. The if statements syntax are

```
if logical expression
    statement;
end


% or the multiple format
 if logical expression
    statement1;
 else
    statement2;
 end
```

3.3.1 *Develop a Scilab function to assign a letter grade for numerical points according to the scale*
$$0 \leq F < 60 \leq C < 75 \leq B < 89 \leq A \leq 100$$

Copy the file grade.sce and check your function for numerical totals: 35, 64, 75, 88.

```
// grade function to assign letter grades
// The input must be a number
function y=grade(X)
if X>=0 & X<=100 //range restriction
if X>= 89 ;
y='A';
elseif X>=75
y='B';
elseif X>= 60
y='C';
else
y='F';
end
else
y='Input is not possible'
end
endfunction
```

For Loops

The for loop syntax is

```
for variable=expression
    statements
end
```

3.3.2 *Find the sum of the first 1000 terms of the alternating harmonic series*

$$\sum_{n=1}^{1000} (-1)^{n-1} \frac{1}{n}$$

and compare it to **ln 2**.

The sum of the series can be accomplished by the following code

```
S=0;
for n=1:10000
  S=S+(-1)^(n-1) /n;
end
S
```

3.3.3 *Construct a function to compute the body mass index for a person with height in inches (**H**) and weight in pounds (**W**), based on the formula*

$$BMI = 703 \times \frac{W}{H^2}$$

and save it as bodymass

```
//          bodymass.sce
// A function to compute Body Mass Index for a person
// Weight(lb) and Height(in)
// BMI=(703)  ((W)/(H^2)

function B=bodymass(w,h) // This function requires two inputs
          B=(703) * (w) / (h^2); //B=bodymassindex
endfunction
```

3.3.4 *Write an sci-file to plot the doubling phenomena that leads to chaos in logistic equation*

$$x_{n+1} = r x_n (1 - x_n)$$

The relevant range of the parameter **r** *is* [2.8,4], *as we increase* **r** *the number of equilibrium points doubles until it become chaotic. For further information refer to your differential equation textbook.*

```
// resolution of bifurcation diagram
m = 200; n = 100;
// initial condition and parameter
x0 = rand(1,m); a = linspace(1,4,m);
// initialize variables
x = zeros(n,m);
x(1,:) = x0;
// step map forward
for i = 1:n
  x(i+1,:) = a.*x(i,:).*(1-x(i,:));
end
// plot
clf
plot(a,x(floor(2*n/3):n,:),'.k','markersize',.1);
xlabel('r'); ylabel('x')
```

3.3.5 *Construct an sci-script to plot flowers in Figure 3.5.*

```
// An SCRIPT-file flower.SCE script to produce
// "flower petal" plots
clf()
t = -%pi:0.01:%pi;
r(1,:) = 2 * sin(5 * t) .^ 2;
r(2,:) = cos(10 * t) .^ 3;
r(3,:) = sin(t) .^ 2;
r(4,:) = 5 * cos(3.5 * t) .^ 3;
for k = 1:4
   m=k;
```

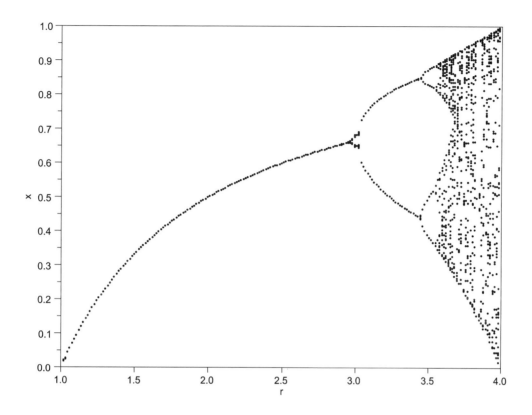

Figure 3.4: The Pitchfork diagram

```
    subplot(2,2,m)
polarplot(t, r(k,:))
end
```

3.3.6 *Create a function that solves the quadratic equation*

$$ax^2 + bx + c = 0.$$

Name the function `quadratic_eq.sce`. *Make sure your function accepts vector input for* a, b, c. *It should be of the form:* [x1 x2]=quad2_eq(a,b,c). *Test your function for*

1. $a = 1, b = -5, c = 6$,   [s1, s2]=quad2_eq (1, -5, 6)

2. $a = 2, b = -1, c = -1$,   [x1, x2]=quad2_eq (2, -1, -1)

3. $a = [1,2,3], b = [-2,0,2], c = [1,1,-3]$: *These represent three different quadratic equations.*

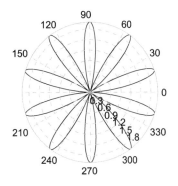 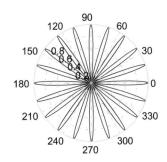

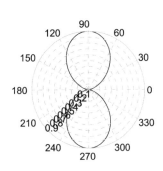 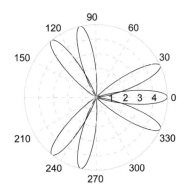

Figure 3.5: Polar flowers

```
// quadratic formula
function  [x1,x2] = quad2_eq(a,b,c);
        x1=(-b+sqrt(b.^2-4*a.*c))./(2*a);
    x2=(-b-sqrt(b.^2-4*a.*c))./(2*a);
endfunction // Run this script
-->[s1,s2]=quad2_eq(1,-5,6)
 s2  =
    2.
 s1  =
    3.
-->[x1, x2]=quad2_eq (2, -1, -1)
 x2  =
  - 0.5
 x1  =
    1.
-->a=[1, 2, 3], b=[ -2, 0, 2], c=[1 , 1, -3]
 a  =
    1.    2.    3.
 b  =
```

```
     - 2.    0.    2.
  c  =
     1.    1.   - 3.
-->[x1,x2]=quad2_eq(a,b,c)
  x2  =
     1.   - 0.70710i  - 1.38742
  x1  =
     1.    0.70710i    0.72075
```

3.3.7 *Create a function sci-file that satisfies the condition for* $-1 < x < 1$, $f(x) = 1$ *and* $f(x) = 0$ *elsewhere. Name the function* `cut_f (x)`. *Test your function as follows:*

```
// Cut Function
function out=cut_f( x);
  if  abs(x) < 1;
  out=1;
  else
  out=0;
  end
endfunction
 x=linspace(-%pi,%pi,200);
 y1=sin(2*x);
 for i=1:200
 y2(i)=sin(2*x(i)).*cut_f(x(i));
 end
 plot(x,y1,'b', x,y2,'r', 'thickness',3)
```

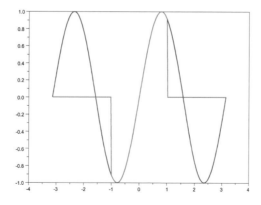

Figure 3.6: The Cut function

3.3.8 *Find eight iterates of* $x_{n+1} = 2x_n + 5, x_0 = -2$ *and print them.*

```
    x(1)=-2;
for i=2:7
    x(i)=2*x(i-1)+5;
end
x' // output in row format
```

3.3.9 *Evaluate the following continued fraction*

$$1 + \cfrac{1}{1 + \cfrac{1}{1 + \cfrac{1}{1 + \cfrac{1}{1 + \cfrac{1}{1 + 1}}}}}$$

Use the following script

```
    c=2;
for i=1:5
    c=1+1/c;
end
c
```

3.4 Homework: Programming, Functions and Scripts

3.4.1 *Create functions to evaluate the following functions (select meaningful names):*

1. $y(x) = x^3 - x$

2. $y(x) = \dfrac{1}{1 + x^2}$

3. $f(x) = cos(x^2)$

and check the functions for $x = 0, 1$

3.4.2 *Create a function to change radians to degrees $y(x) = \dfrac{180}{\pi} x$ and check the function for $x = \pi/2, \pi/3$*

3.4.3 *Create a function to compute the area of the triangle $A(h, b) = \dfrac{hb}{2}$ and check the function for $h = 2, b = 10$*

3.4.4 *The harmonic series $\sum_{n=1}^{\infty} \dfrac{1}{n}$ is divergent. Write a script file to sum the series*

1. $\sum_{n=1}^{100} \dfrac{1}{n}$

2. $\sum_{n=1}^{1000} \dfrac{1}{n}$

3. $\sum_{n=1}^{100000} \dfrac{1}{n}$

3.4.5 *The series $S_n = \sum_{k=1}^{n} \dfrac{6}{k^2}$ is convergent. Find $\sqrt{S_n}$ for different values of n:*

1. $n = 100$

2. $n = 1000$

3. $n = 10000$

4. $n = 100000$

Divide the above sums by the value π. What is your conclusion?

3.4.6 *Evaluate the following continued fraction*

$$1 + \cfrac{1}{1 + \cfrac{1}{2 + \cfrac{1}{3 + \cfrac{1}{4 + \cfrac{1}{5 + \cfrac{1}{6 + \cfrac{1}{7 + \cfrac{1}{8 + \cfrac{1}{9 + \cfrac{1}{10 + 1}}}}}}}}}}$$

4 2-D Graphics

Graphics are integral part of Scilab environment. Plotting and simulation the computational results is made simple with few Scilab commands. These commands are divided into two-dimensional, three dimensional graphics, coloring techniques and simulation. There is the general plot function and the more versatile functions plot2d.

4.1 Two-dimensional graphics

Scilab provides plotting capabilities with x-y and polar coordinates. It offers several functions to animate 2-D curves and vector field plots. The most common plotting commands are

plot	2D plot
fplot2d	2D plot of a curve defined by a function
polarplot	Plot polar coordinates
paramfplot2d	animated plot of a 2D parametrized curve.
comet	2D comet animated plot.
champ	2D vector field plot
champ1	2D vector field plot with colored arrows

The plot function is the basic command to graph vectors and arrays: plot(y) , plot(x,y) .
In Scilab, you can change the appearance of each plot by selecting the color, the style, the marking and many other options. Below we list some of these options.

```
// Plot Options to be used with plotting curves
// --------------------
// x=1:10; // Interval
//plot(x,sin(x),'colo','red','linest','-.','marker','>',...
//'markeredg','cyan','markerFace','yellow','markersize',5)
// 'thickness'      2
// Axis Properties
```

```
//xtitle('Plot of three functions','x label','y label')
//plot(x, y, 'x axis label', 'y axis label', 'title of plot')
```

Spec.	Marker Type
.	Point
o	Circle
*	Star
+	Plus
x	Cross
s	Square
d	Diamond
>	Right-pointing triangle
<	Left-pointing triangle

Specifier	Line style
–	solid line
––	dashed line
:	dotted line
–.	dash-dotted line

Spec.	Color
y	Yellow
r	Red
b	Blue
g	Green
k	Black
c	Cyan
m	Magenta
w	White

4.1.1 *Multiple plots with different line specifications.*

```
clf();
x=(0:0.05:2*%pi);
y1=sin(x)-3; y2=sin(2*x)-1; y4=sin(4*x)+1; y8=sin(8*x)+3;
plot(x,y1,'*r', x,y2,'-.ob', x,y4,'--dg',x,y8,'k')
title('Multiple plots','fontsize',5)
```

4.1.2 *Given the vectors*
$x = [-4 \quad -3 \quad -2 \quad -1 \quad 0 \quad 1 \quad 2 \quad 3 \quad 4]$ *and*
$y = [8 \quad 4 \quad 1 \quad -1 \quad 3 \quad -1 \quad 2 \quad 3 \quad 6]$
Perform the following:

1. plot(x,y)

2. plot(x,y,'r')

3. plot(x,y,'*m')

4. plot(y,x,'dc')

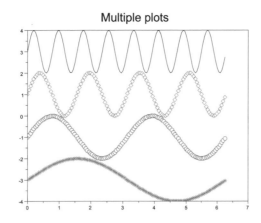

Figure 4.1: Multiple plots

4.1.1 Graphs of Functions of a Single Variable

4.1.3 *Graph the function*

$$y = 2x - 1$$

on $[-3,3] \times [-5,5]$ *and show a system of coordinates in the origin with all titles.*

```
x=-3:.1:3;
y=2*x-1;
isoview(-1,1,-1,1)\\For square window
plot(x,y,'r')
xsegs([0,0], [-5,5], 2); // Draw a segment as y-axis in blue
xsegs([-3,3], [0,0], 2); // Draw a segment as y-axis in blue
xtitle(' Straight Line', 'x-axis', 'y-axis');
```

4.1.4 *Graph the function*

$$y = \frac{sin(2x)}{x}, \qquad x \neq 0$$

on $[-25,25]$

```
function y=fn(x); y= sin(2*x)./x; endfunction // Note the dot division
x=-25:.02:25;
x=x+%eps; // Why do we need to add eps?
//plot2d(x,fn(x));
plot(x,fn(x),'r','thickness',3) // Note the name of the function fn(x)
title('$y=\dfrac{\sin(2x)}{x}$','fontsize',3)
```

4.1.5 *Graph the function* $y = x^{1/3}(x-2)^2(x+1)^{1/3}$ *on* $[-1.5,3]$

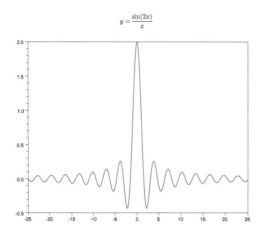

Figure 4.2

```
function y=f(x); y= x.^(1/3).*(x-2).^(2).*(x+1).^(1/3); endfunction
x=-1.5:.02:3;
plot(x,f(x),'k','thickness',3)
title('$y=x^{1/3}(x-2)^2(x+1)^{1/3}$','fontsize',3)
```

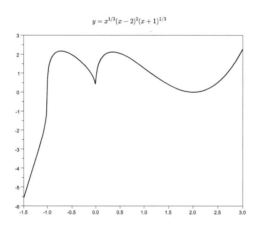

Figure 4.3

4.1.2 Parametric and Polar Plots

Curves in parametric equations

$$x = x(t), \qquad y = y(t), \qquad a \le t \le b$$

can be graphed using the function `plot(x,y)` and curves in polar coordinates

$$r = f(\theta), \qquad \alpha \le \theta \le \beta$$

can be graphed using the function `polarplot(\theta,r)`. Furthermore, Every equation in polar format can be written in a parametric format. For example, the last equation can be expressed as follows

$$x = f(\theta)\cos(\theta), \qquad y = f(\theta)\sin(\theta), \qquad \alpha \le \theta \le \beta$$

4.1.6 *Graph the parametric equations*

$$x(t) = t + 3|\sin(3t)|$$

$$y(t) = t + 3\cos(4t)$$

for $-\pi < t < \pi$. Use the two dimensional simulation command comet to follow the motion path.

```
t=-%pi:.01:%pi;
x=t+3*abs(sin(3*t));
y=t+3*cos(4*t);
plot(x,y,'b','thickness',3)
title('Parametric curve','fontsize',3)
\\ For simulation
clf
comet(x,y)
```

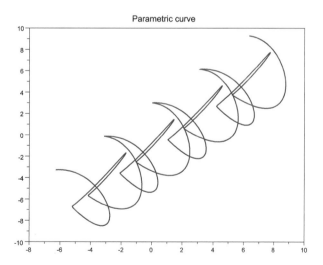

Figure 4.4: Parametric Curve

4.1.7 *Graph the parametric equations of cardioid*

$$x(t) = (1 - \sin(t))\cos(t)$$

$$y(t) = (1 - \sin(t))\sin(t)$$

for $-\pi < t < \pi$. Fill the figure in red color.

```
t=-%pi:.01:%pi;
x=(1-sin(t)).*cos(t);
y=(1-sin(t)).*sin(t);
//plot(x,y,'r','thickness',3)

 plot2d(0,0,-1,'010','',[-2,-2.5,5,1.5]);
    xset('color',5)
    xfpoly(x,y)//Fill the region with color
 // Add another heart
   xfpoly(x+2.5,y-.5)
```

Figure 4.5: Two Hearts

4.1.8 *Graph the the polar equation*

$$r = \theta \sin(\theta)$$

for $-8\pi < \theta < 8\pi$

```
theta=-8*%pi:.01:8*%pi;
r=theta .* sin(theta);
polarplot(theta,r)
title('Polar curve','fontsize',3)
```

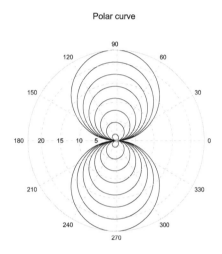

Figure 4.6: Polar Curve

4.1.9 *Graph the butterfly curve for* $0 < t < 12\pi$ *given parametrically:*

$$x(t) = \sin(t)(e^{\cos(t)} - 2\cos(4t) - \sin(t/12)^5)$$

$$y(t) = \cos(t)(e^{\cos(t)} - 2\cos(4t) - \sin(t/12)^5)$$

```
t=0:.01:12*%pi;
ct=cos(t);
p2=exp(ct)-2*cos(4*t)-sin(t/12).^5;
x=sin(t).*p2;
y=ct.*p2;
plot(x,y)
xtitle('Butterfly Curve')
```

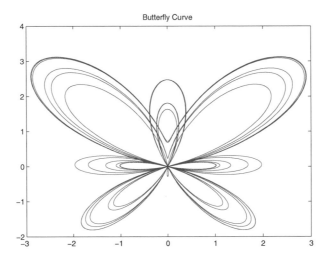

Figure 4.7: Butterfly Curve

4.1.3 Combining plots

It is possible to include several plots in one window. subplot divides the window into array of several smaller plots. subplot(m , n, r) command has three parameters:

1. *m*: the first number of plot rows

2. *n*: the second number of plot columns

3. *r*: the third number is the location of the plot by counting left to right and then continue counting second row left to right.

4.1.10 *Graph the the first six Bessel functions J_n, $0 \le n \le 5$ in a 2×3 figure.*

```
x= 0: 0.05 : 30;
 for n= 1:6
     subplot(3,2,n)
     plot (x, besselj(n-1, x),'k', 'thickness',3)
 end
```

4.1.11 *Subdivide the figure into two rows and one column. Graph $y = x\sin(6x)$ on $[-6,6]$ in the upper row, and graph $y = x^2 - 5$ using the round function over $[-3,3]$.*

```
clf
x1=-6:.1:6;
x2=-3:.01:3;
subplot(2,1,1)
```

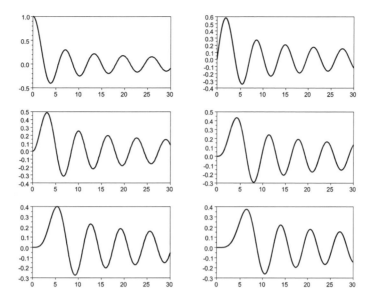

Figure 4.8: Bessel Functions

```
plot(x1,x1.*sin(6*x1),'thickness',3)
title('$x\sin(x)$','fontsize',3)
subplot(2,1,2)
plot(x2,round(x2.^2-5),'thickness',3)
title('$x^2-5$','fontsize',3)
```

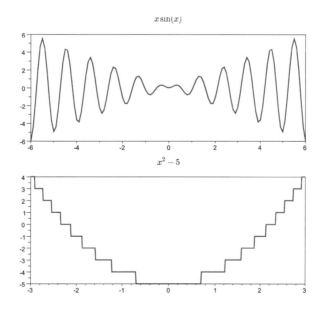

Figure 4.9: Two level figure

4.1.4 2-dimensional plots and Annotation

1. Graph the function $y = 3x - x^3$ on $[-3, 2]$ with step size .1. Add a title and labels to your plot. Add grid and axis $[-43], [-45]$. Use pause between commands.

   Solution:

   ```
   // date and name
   clf()
   x = -3:0.1:2;
   y = 3*x-(x).^3;
   plot(x,y, 'thickness',3);
   // Add labels and titles
   xtitle('Cube Function' , 'X', 'Y', boxed =1 );
   a=get('current_axes');//get the handle of the newly created axes
   a.data_bounds=[-4,-4;3,5]; // left corner and upper right corner
   ```

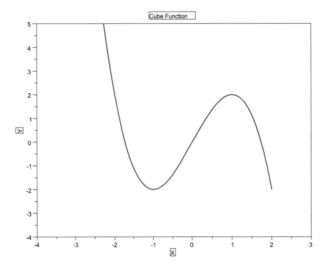

   Figure 4.10: Example 1

   □

2. Use the values of the function y from previous example and plot it in red color with linewidth 3 and on the same system of coordinates plot the five rigid transformations: up, down, left, right by five units and x-reflection in different color on axis $[-8, 8], [-8, 8]$. plot y versus x on the same figure and find the type of symmetry compared to x versus y.

   Solution:

   ```
   // date and name
   clf
   x = -3:0.1:2;
   ```

```
y = 3*x-(x).^3;
plot(x,y,'r', 'thickness',4)
plot(x+5,y,'g', 'thickness',3)
plot(x-5,y,'b', 'thickness',3)
plot(x,y+5,'c',x,y-5,'m', 'thickness',3)
plot(x,-y,'k', 'thickness',3)
//axis([-8 8 -8 8])
plot(y,x,'y', 'thickness',3)
a=get("current_axes");//get the handle of the newly created axes
a.data_bounds=[-8,-8;8,8]; // left corner and upper right corner
title('Rigid Transformations','fontsize',3)
```

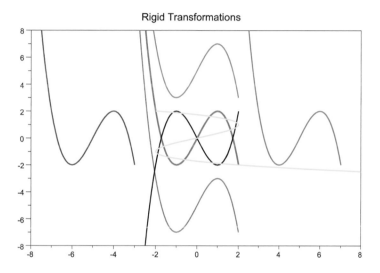

Figure 4.11: Example 2

$\square$

3. Plot the functions: $|\sin(x)|$, $x\sin(x)$, $\cos(1/x)$, $\cos(x)^5$ on $-\pi < x < \pi$ with step size 0.01π. Plot on same figure with different colors and markers and add legends.

Solution:

```
// date and name
clf
x = -%pi:.01*%pi:%pi;
plot(x,abs(sin(x)),'-r');
plot(x,x.*sin(2*x),'--b');
plot(x,cos(1./(x)),':g');
plot(x,cos(x).^5,'oc');
//legend('|(sin(x)|','xsin(2x)','cos(1/x)','cos(x)^5');
//legends(['|(sin(x)|';'xsin(2x)';'cos(1/x)'; 'cos(x)^5']);
```

$\square$

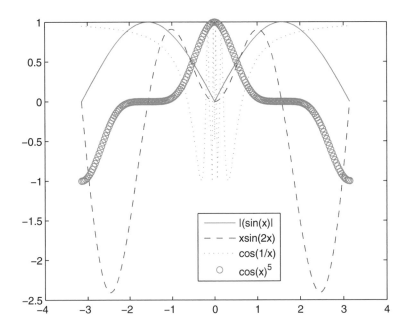

Figure 4.12: Example 3

4. Use subplot **2** to plot a triangle in the upper left cell, a square in the upper right, a circle in the lower left cell and the three graphs together in the lower right cell.

Solution:

```
// Construct the x and y  vector coordinates
clf
x_s = [-3  3 3 -3 -3]; // square
y_s = [-3 -3 3  3 -3];
x_c = 3*cos([0:%pi/50:2*%pi]);//outer circle
y_c = 3*sin([0:%pi/50:2*%pi]);
x_t = 3*cos([%pi/2 %pi/2+2*%pi/3 %pi/2+4*%pi/3 %pi/2]);//triangle
y_t = 3*sin([%pi/2 %pi/2+2*%pi/3 %pi/2+4*%pi/3 %pi/2]);
x_cc = (3)/2*cos([0:%pi/50:2*%pi]);//inner circle
y_cc = (3)/2*sin([0:%pi/50:2*%pi]);
//Plot the triangle in the upper left pane
subplot(2,2,1)
plot(x_t,y_t,'b');
a=get("current_axes");
a.data_bounds=[-4,-4;4,4];
//axis([-4 4 -4 4]); axis equal;
xtitle('Triangle');
//Plot the square in the upper right pane
subplot(2,2,2)
```

```
plot(x_s,y_s,'r');
a=get("current_axes");
a.data_bounds=[-4,-4;4,4];
//axis([-4 4 -4 4]); axis equal;
xtitle('Square');

//Plot the circle in the lower left pane
subplot(2,2,3)
plot(x_c,y_c,'g');
plot(x_cc,y_cc,'k')
a=get("current_axes");
a.data_bounds=[-4,-4;4,4];
xtitle('Circle');

//Plot all figures  in the lower right pane
subplot(2,2,4)
plot(x_s,y_s,'r');

plot(x_c,y_c,'g');
plot(x_t,y_t,'b');
plot(x_cc,y_cc,'k');
a=get("current_axes");
a.data_bounds=[-4,-4;4,4];
xtitle('Combination Plot');
```

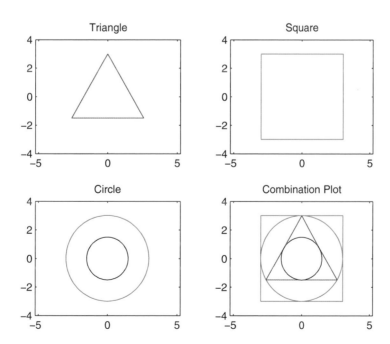

Figure 4.13: Example 4

□

5. Graph the polar coordinate curve

$$r = 0.5 + \cos(2\theta), \qquad 0 \le \theta \le 2\pi$$

in subplot(2,2,1) and express the same curve in parametric form and graph it in subplot (2,2,2). Similarly, Graph the rose

$$r = \cos(16\theta/13), \qquad 0 \le \theta \le 26\pi$$

in subplot (2,2,3) and its parametric format in subplot(2,2,4).

Solution:

```
// Polar and parametric curves
clf
 t = 0:.01:2*%pi;
 r = .5 + cos(2*t);

subplot(2,2,1)
polarplot(t,r)
xtitle('Polar plot')

subplot(2,2,2)
x=r.*cos(t);
y=r.*sin(t);
plot(x,y);
xtitle('Tie')


 t = 0:.01:26*%pi;
 r = cos(16*t/13);

subplot(2,2,3)
polarplot(t,r)
xtitle('Polar Rose')

subplot(2,2,4)
x=r.*cos(t);
y=r.*sin(t);
plot(x,y);
xtitle('Rose')
```

□

6. **Colorful geometric shapes**. Graph regular polygons shapes filled with colors on the same figure: Triangle, Square, Pentagon, ... , Circle.

Solution:

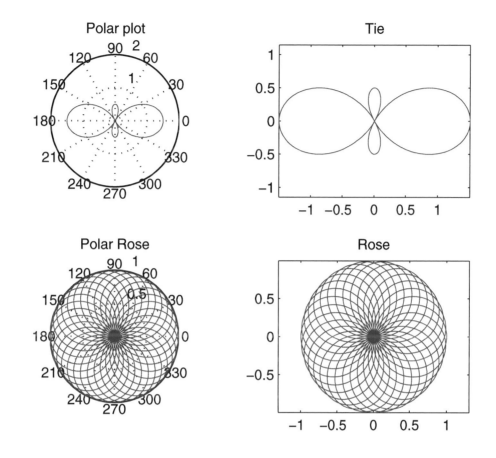

Figure 4.14: Example 5

```
// Geometric shapes
clf
x_3=cos([0:2*%pi/3:2*%pi]);//triangle: 2pi/3
y_3=sin([0:2*%pi/3:2*%pi]);
x_4=cos([0:%pi/2:2*%pi]);//square: pi/2
y_4=sin([0:%pi/2:2*%pi]);


x_5=cos([0:2*%pi/5:2*%pi]);//pentagon: 2pi/5
y_5=sin([0:2*%pi/5:2*%pi]);
x_6=cos([0:2*%pi/6:2*%pi]); //hexagon: 2pi/6
y_6=sin([0:2*%pi/6:2*%pi]);
x_7=cos([0:2*%pi/7:2*%pi]); //septagon: 2pi/7
y_7=sin([0:2*%pi/7:2*%pi]);
x_8=cos([0:2*%pi/8:2*%pi]); //octagon: 2pi/8
y_8=sin([0:2*%pi/8:2*%pi]);


x=0:.01:2*%pi;
x_c=cos(x); //circle
```

```
y_c=sin(x);
x_w=0:.02:6;y_w=exp(-.4*x_w).*sin(4*x_w); // wavy function

//Creating shapes with colors on a figure 20 by 20
//Shift the coordinates to arrange shape on the figure
//colors: c= 1 black; 2 blue; 3 green; 4 cyan; 5  red, and so on up to 40 co

plot2d(0,0,-1,"010"," ",[0,0,20,20])//last vector specifies the domain

xset("color",2)
xfpoly(4+2*x_3, 16+2*y_3);

xset("color",5)
xfpoly(10+2*x_4, 16+2*y_4);

xset("color",3)
xfpoly(16+3*x_5, 16+3*y_5);

xset("color",7)
xfpoly(4+2*x_6, 10+2*y_6);

xset("color",6)
xfpoly(10+2*x_7, 10+2*y_7);

xset("color",18)
xfpoly(16+3*x_8, 10+3*y_8);
xset("color",13)
xfpoly(4+2*x_c, 4+2*y_c);

xset("color",19)
xfpoly(10+1*x_c, 4+2*y_c);

xset("color",1)
xfpoly(16+3*x_c, 3.5+3*y_c);

xset("color",22)
xfpoly(16+3*x_6, 3.5+3*y_6);

xset("color",32)
xfpoly(16+3*x_4, 3.5+3*y_4);

//fill(8+2*x_w, 4+2*y_w,y_w.*x_w);
xtitle('Colorful geometric figures')
```

Colorful geometric figures

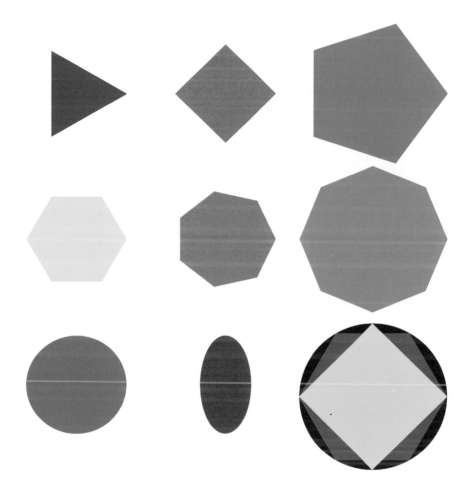

Figure 4.15: Example 6

4.2 Homework: 2-d curves

4.2.1 *Use an increment of* **0.02** *for the interval* $0 \le x \le 2\pi$ *then plot the function* $y = \sin(15x)\sin(3x)$. *Add title and labels to the plot*

4.2.2 *1. Subdivide a figure into two rows and one column*

2. In the top row, plot $y = \tanh(2x)$ *on the interval* $-4 \le x \le 4$ *in increments of* **0.1**.

3. Add a title and labels to the plot

4. In the lower row, plot x *versus* $y = \tan(x)$ *on the same range*

5. Add a title and labels to the plot

4.2.3 *Subdivide a figure into four regions and plot one function in each subplot with titles and as follows*

1. $y1 = \sin(x)$ *in red and solid*

2. $y2 = \sin(2x)$ *in blue and dashed*

3. $y3 = \sqrt[3]{3x - x^3}$ *in green and dotted*

4. $y4 = 9x^2 - x^4$ *in yellow and star*

on interval $[-\pi, \pi]$ *in increments of* **0.1**

4.2.4 *Plot the functions on the same system of coordinates*

1. the Gauss curve $y = e^{-x^2/2}$

2. the Cauchy curve $y = -\dfrac{2}{1 + x^2}$

for the interval $[-3, 3]$ *in increments of* **0.02**

4.2.5 *Parametric curves*: *Subdivide a figure into four regions and plot one curve in each region, include titles*

1. $x = 3\sin^5 t, \quad y = 3\cos^5 t$ *for* $0 \le t \le 2\pi$

2. $x = 9\cos t - 3\cos 4t, \quad y = 9\cos t - 3\sin 4t$ *for* $0 \le t \le 2\pi$

3. $x = 3t - 2\sin t, \quad y = 3 - 2\cos t$ *for* $-8 \le t \le 8$

4. $x = 2t - 3\sin t, \quad y = 2 - 3\cos t$ *for* $-8 \le t \le 8$

4.2.6 *Curves in polar coordinates*: *Subdivide a figure into two regions and plot one curve in each region, include titles*

1. $r = 2\sin^2\theta\tan^2\theta$ *for* $-\pi/3 \le \theta \le \pi/3$

2. $r = \dfrac{4}{1+\sin^2\theta}$ *for* $0 \le \theta \le 2\pi$

5   3-D Graphics

5.1   Three-dimensional functions

Drawing a three-dimensional graph of a data set or a function can lead to a deeper understanding of the behavior of the data. Manipulating the colors is essential to seeing complicated shapes in three and in four dimensional functions. Each file in the following problems serves as a model to graph and to gain better understanding, you are advised to change one parameter or option in each line and observe its effect.

The param3d, plot3d, surf commands are the basic functions to plot 3-dimensional curves and surfaces. The common format of these functions are

param3d(x,y,z)   plots 3-d curves

comet3d(x,y,z)   animated 3-d curves

plot3d(x,y,z)   plots surfaces

surf(x,y,z)   plots surfaces

fplot3d(x,y,f)   plots surfaces

champ(x,y,z)   2-D vector field

contour(x,y,z)   plots a contour plot

mesh(x,y,z)   plots a meshed surface

5.2   Three Dimensional Curves

Three dimensional curves are assumed to be written in parametric form that is

$$x = f(t)$$
$$y = g(t)$$
$$z = h(t)$$

for a parameter $t \in [a, b]$. The graphing of three dimensional line plots involves:

1. Creating a parametric vector over the interval $[a, b]$ say $t(i)$.

2. Creating the three vectors x(i), y(i), z(i) from the given formula.

3. Using param3d(x , y, z) and annotate the curve and use comet3d(x , y, z) to simulate the motion of a particle along the curve.

5.2.1 *Animate the spiral conic helix*

$$x = (t/10)\cos(t), \qquad y = (t/10)\sin(t), \qquad z = t$$

for $-10\pi \le t \le 10\pi$ *with step size* $.01\pi$ *and graph it.*

Solution:

```
clf()
t = -10*%pi:0.01:10*%pi;
x = (t/10).*cos(t);
y = (t/10).*sin(t);
z = t;
comet3d(x,y,z);//Animation
clf()
param3d(x,y,z,30, 20, "X@Y@Z" );// View and axes labels
a=gce();// the handle on the 3D
a.thickness = 3;
title('Conic Helix','fontsize',3);
```
□

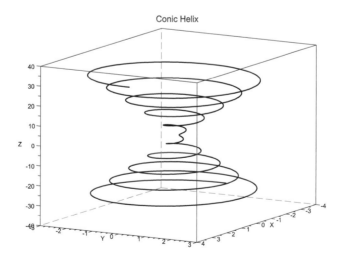

Figure 5.1: Conic Helix

5.2.2 *Graph and animate the circular helix*

$$x = \cos(3t), \qquad y = \sin(3t), \qquad z = t$$

for $0\pi \le t \le 4\pi$ with step size $.001\pi$.

Solution:

```
clf
//Circular Helix
t =-0:%pi/1000:4*%pi;
param3d(sin(10*t),cos(10*t),t,35,45,"X@Y@Z",[2,0]);// axes and Box off
```
□

5.2.3 *Graph the spring torus*

$$x = (4 + \sin(80t))\cos(3t), \qquad y = (4 + \sin(80t))\sin(3t), \qquad z = \cos(80t)$$

for $0\pi \le t \le 4\pi$ with step size $.001\pi$ and superimpose three concentrated tori.

Solution:

```
clf
//Spring Torus
t =-0:%pi/1000:4*%pi;
x=(4+sin(80*t)).*cos(3*t);
y=(4+sin(80*t)).*sin(3*t);
z=cos(80*t);
param3d(x,y,z)
e=gce(); //the handle on the 3D polyline
e.foreground=color('blue');

x=(6+sin(80*t)).*cos(3*t);
y=(6+sin(80*t)).*sin(3*t);
param3d(y,z,x)
e=gce(); //the handle on the 3D polyline
e.foreground=color('red');

x=(8+sin(80*t)).*cos(3*t);
y=(8+sin(80*t)).*sin(3*t);
param3d(z,y,x)
e=gce(); //the handle on the 3D polyline
e.foreground=color('green');

xtitle('Concentrated Tori')
a=gca() //get the current axes
a.box="off";
```

Concentrated Tori

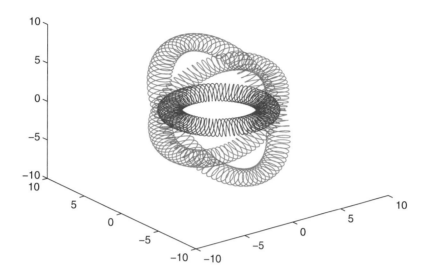

Figure 5.2: Concentrated Tori

□

5.2.4 *The Borremean rings are topological knots are given parametrically by:*

$$x = -a + \cos(t); y = \sin(t); z = b\cos(3t); Left\ ring$$

$$x = a + \cos(t); y = \sin(t); z = b\cos(3t); Right\ ring$$

$$x = \cos(t); y = \sin(t) - \sin(\pi/3); z = b\cos(3t); Left\ ring$$

*where $a = 0.5$, $b = 0.2$, $0 < t < 2\pi$. Graph these rings and **view them from different angles**.*

Solution:

```
clf
// Borromean Rings Link
a=0.5; b=0.2;
t=0:.01:2*%pi;
// Left ring
x=-a+cos(t); y= sin(t); z=b* cos( 3*t);
param3d(x,y,z)
e=gce(); e.foreground=color('blue');
e.thickness = 4;
```

```
// Right ring
x=a+cos(t); y= sin(t); z=b* cos( 3*t);
param3d(x,y,z)
e=gce(); e.foreground=color('red');
e.thickness = 6;
// Lower ring
x=cos(t); y= sin(t) - sin(%pi/3) ; z=b* cos( 3*t);
param3d(x,y,z,15, 80)
e=gce(); e.foreground=color('green');
e.thickness = 8;
a=gca() //get the current axes
a.box="off";
```

□

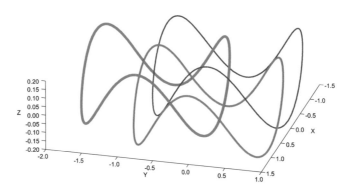

Figure 5.3: Borremean Rings

5.2.5 *Graph the Trefoil topological knot which is given parametrically by:*

$$x = \cos(pt)(r + \cos(qt))$$
$$y = \sin(pt)(r + \cos(qt))$$
$$z = \sin(qt)$$

where $p = 2, \quad q = 3, \quad r = 3, \quad 0 < t < 2\pi.$

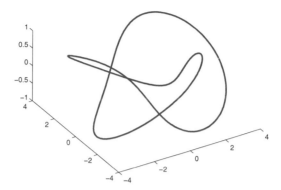

Figure 5.4: Trefoil Knot

5.3   Three Dimensional Surfaces

There are two ways of describing surfaces. The explicit format in which the z coordinate is given by a function of x and y. and the parametric format, in which the coordinates x, y, and z are given as functions of two other parameters.

Graphing three dimensional surfaces which are given by explicit equations $z = f(x, y)$ over a domain is accomplished as follows:

1. Discretize the rectangular domain as two vector

2. Define a function of the surface

3. Evaluate the over the domain z = f(x, y)

4. Graph the surface using one of the commands: plot3d(x,y,z), fplot3d(x,y,f), surf(x,y,z)

5. Use contour plots to draw level curves using: contour(x,y,z,n)

6. There are optional commands for color, axes, and annotations

5.3.1 *Graph the surface*

$$z = x^3 - 3xy^2$$

known as the monkey saddle using the commands fplot3d(x,y,f), plot3d(x,y,z), surf(x,y,z) *, and plot its contours over the domain* $[-3, 3] \times [-3, 3]$.

Solution:

```
//Monkey Saddle Surface
x=-3:0.1:3; y=x; // Discretize
function z=monkey_surf(x,y),z=x^3-3*x*y^2, endfunction
```

```
subplot(2,2,1)
fplot3d(x,y,monkey_surf)
f=get("current_figure");//get the handle of the parent figure
f.color_map=hsvcolormap(32);// red, yellow, green, blue

subplot(2,2,2)
contour(x,y, monkey_surf,15)// 15 uniform level curves

subplot(2,2,3)
t=linspace(-3,3,30);
z=feval(t,t,monkey_surf);
[xx,yy,zz]=genfac3d(t,t,z);
surf(xx,yy,zz,'facecol','red','edgecol','yellow")

subplot(2,2,4)
t=linspace(-3,3,30);
z=feval(t,t,monkey_surf);
plot3d1(t,t,z,-5,80) // different view (angles)                 □
```

5.3.2 *Graph the surface*

$$z = -\sin(x^2 + y^2)$$

over the domain $[-1.25, 1.25] \times [-1.25, 1.25]$. **Use the figure editor property to drop the box and the axes and explore the colors.** *Can you give a plausible name to this surface?*

Solution:

```
x=-1.15:.1:1.15; y=x;
function z=f(x,y) ;z=-sin(x^2+y^2);endfunction
z=feval(x,y,f);
subplot(1,2,1)
plot3d(x,y,z)
subplot(1,2,2)
plot3d1(x,y,z)
```

□

5.3.3 *Graph the following surfaces using* fplot3d *function on a two by two figure:*

$$z_1 = \sin(x)\cos(y), \qquad z_2 = \sqrt{x^2 + y^2}\sin(x + y)$$

$$z_3 = \sin(x + y)/\sqrt{x^2 + y^2}, \qquad z4 = (x^2 + 4y^2)e^{-x^2 - y^2}$$

over the square $[-2\pi, 2\pi] \times [-2\pi, 2\pi]$.

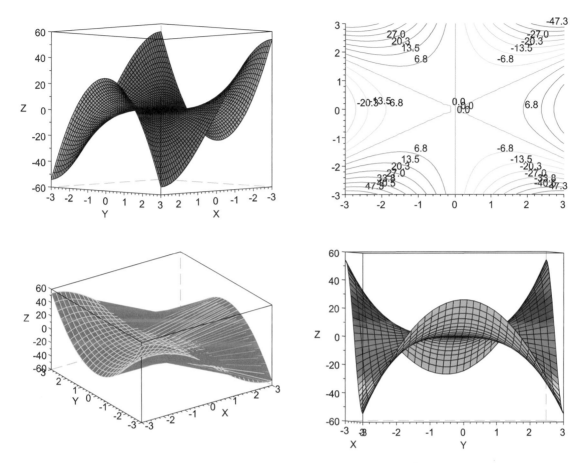

Figure 5.5: Monkey Saddle Surface

5.3.4 *Graph the surface*

$$z = 4e^{-(x^2+y^2)} + (x^2+y^2)/4$$

on the square $[-2,2]^2$. *Use fplot3d, contour and color commands.*

Solution:

```
// date and name
scf(1);
x=-2:.2:2; y=x;
function z=f(x,y),z=4*exp(-(x^2+y^2))+(x^2+y^2)/4;endfunction
fplot3d(x,y,f);

//Contour plots with 10 levels
scf(2);
contour(x,y,f,10)

scf(3);
```

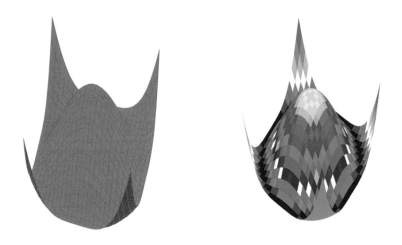

Figure 5.6: Sombrero Surface

```
z=feval(x,y,f);
// same plot using facets computed by genfac3d
[xx,yy,zz]=genfac3d(x,y,z);
surf(xx,yy,zz,'facecol','r','edgecol','m');

// Multicolors
scf(4);
plot3d([xx xx],[yy yy],list([zz zz+4],[4*ones(1,400) 5*ones(1,400)]))
```

□

5.4   Vector Field Plots

The partial derivatives of a surface can be obtained by the gradient function. The gradient vector field can be plotted with arrows pointing to increasing and decreasing values. champ plots arrows with components (u, v) at the points (x, y).

5.4.1 *Plot the gradient vector field of the surface*

$$z = x^3/2 + xy + y^3/2$$

on the square $[-2, 2] \times [-2, 2]$ *using the champ function.*

Solution:

```
clf
x=-2: .2: 2; y=x;
function z=fx(x,y),z=1.5*x^2+y;endfunction
function z=fy(x,y),z=x+1.5*y^2;endfunction
function z=f(x,y),z=x^3/2+x*y+y^3/2;endfunction
zx=feval(x,y,fx); zy=feval(x,y,fy);
champ1(x,y,zx,zy)
contour(x,y,f,10)
xtitle('Gradient flow on z=(x^3+y^3)/2+xy')
```

□

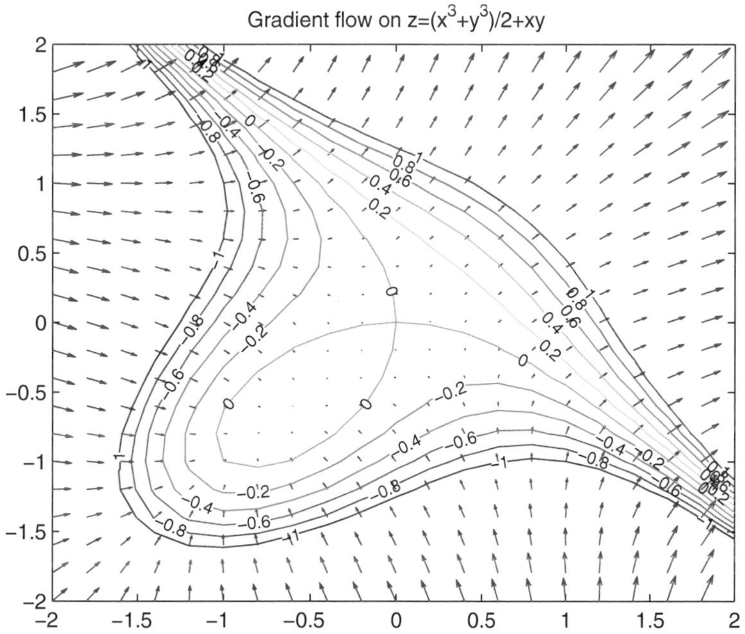

Figure 5.7: Gradient Field

5.4.2 *Plot the vector field* $(x, -y)$ *of the surface*

$$z = x^2/2 - y^2/2$$

on the square $[-2, 2] \times [-2, 2]$ *using the champ function, and plot* **10** *level curves of the surface on the vector field.*

Solution:

```
clf
x=-2: .2: 2; y=x;
function z=fx(x,y),z=x;endfunction
function z=fy(x,y),z=-y;endfunction
function z=f(x,y),z=x^2-y^2;endfunction
zx=feval(x,y,fx); zy=feval(x,y,fy);
champ1(x,y,zx,zy)
contour(x,y,f,10)
title('Vector Field Plot (x,-y) and Level Curves of  z=x^2/2-y^2/2')
```

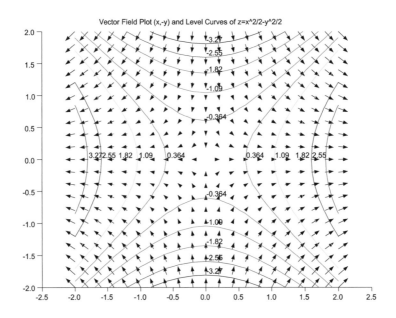

Figure 5.8: Vector Field

5.4.3 *Plot the contour plot of the surface*

$$f(x, y) = x^2 - 2xy + y - y^2$$

on the square $[-4, 4] \times [-4, 4]$ *with its gradient vector field.*

5.5 Surfaces in parametric form

Surfaces given in parametric form can be plotted using Scilab functions as demonstrated in the following examples:

5.5.1 *Plot the following parametric surfaces:*

1. *Circular cylinder:* $x = \cos v$, $\quad y = \sin v$, $\quad z = u$ *on* $[-\pi, \pi] \times [-\pi, \pi]$

2. *Circular cone:* $x = u \cos v$, $\quad y = u \sin v$, $\quad z = u$ *on* $[-\pi, \pi] \times [-\pi, \pi]$

3. *Circular helix:* $x = u \cos v$, $\quad y = u \sin v$, $\quad z = v$ *on* $[-\pi, \pi] \times [-\pi, \pi]$

4. *Twisted cone:*
   $x = (u - \sin u) \cos v$, $\quad y = (1 - \cos u) \sin v$, $\quad z = u$ *on* $[-\pi, \pi] \times [-\pi, \pi]$

5. *Twisted horn:*
   $x = (1 - u)(3 + \cos v) \cos(4\pi u)$, $\quad y = (1 - u)(3 + \cos v) \sin(4\pi u)$, $\quad z = 3u + (1 - u) \sin v$ *on* $[-1, 1] \times [-1, 1]$

6. *Twisted cylinder:*
   $x = (2 + \sin v) \cos u$, $\quad y = (2 + \sin v) \sin u$, $\quad z = u + \cos v$ *on* $[-\pi, \pi] \times [-\pi, \pi]$

7. *Miobus strip:*
   $x = 2 \cos v + u \cos(v/2)$, $\quad y = 2 \sin v + u \cos(v/2)$, $\quad z = u \sin(v/2)$ *on* $[-.5, .5] \times [0, 2\pi]$

8. *Dini's surface:*
   $x = \cos u \sin v$, $\quad y = \sin u \sin v$, $\quad z = \cos v + \log(\tan(v/2)) + u/(2\pi)$ *on* $[2\pi, 6\pi] \times [0, \pi/2]$

Solution:

```
//Parametric surfaces
clf
//circular cylinder
figure(1);
subplot(2,2,1);
st=.1;
function [x,y,z]=f(u,v); x=cos(v);y=sin(v);z=u;endfunction
u1=-%pi:st:%pi+st;v1=u1;
[x1,y1,z1]=eval3dp(f,u1,v1);
plot3d1(x1,y1,z1);
xtitle('Circular cylinder ')

// circularity cone
subplot(2,2,2)
st=.1;
function [x,y,z]=f2(u,v); x=u.*cos(v);y=u.*sin(v);z=u;endfunction
u1=-%pi:st:%pi+st;v1=u1;
```

```
[x1,y1,z1]=eval3dp(f2,u1,v1);
plot3d1(x1,y1,z1);
xtitle('Circular cone ')


//#3 circular helix
subplot(2,2,3)
st=.1;
function [x,y,z]=f2(u,v); x=u.*cos(v);y=u.*sin(v);z=v;endfunction
u1=-%pi:st:%pi+st;v1=u1;
[x1,y1,z1]=eval3dp(f2,u1,v1);
//plot3d1(x1,y1,z1);
plot3d(x1,y1,z1)
xtitle('Circular helix ')



//#4 twisted cone
subplot(2,2,4)
st=.1;

function [x,y,z]=f2(u,v); x=(u-sin(u)).*cos(v);y=(1-cos(u)).*sin(v);z=u;endfunct
u1=-%pi:st:%pi+st;v1=u1;
[x1,y1,z1]=eval3dp(f2,u1,v1);
plot3d1(x1,y1,z1);
//plot3d(x1,y1,z1)
xtitle('Twisted cone ')



//#5 Twisted horn
figure(2)
subplot(2,2,1)
st=.02;

function [x,y,z]=f2(u,v);
x=(1-u).*(3+cos(v)).*cos(4*%pi*u);
y=(1-u).*(3+cos(v)).*sin(4*%pi*u);
z=3*u+(1-u).*sin(v);
endfunction

u1=-1:st:1+st;v1=u1;

[x1,y1,z1]=eval3dp(f2,u1,v1);
plot3d(x1,y1,z1);

xtitle('Twisted horn  ')
```

```
//  twisted cylinder
subplot(2,2,2)
st=.1;
function [x,y,z]=f2(u,v);
x=(2+sin(v)).*cos(u);
y=(2+sin(v)).*sin(u);
z=u+cos(v);
endfunction

u1=-%pi:st:3*%pi+st;v1=-%pi:st:%pi+st;

[x1,y1,z1]=eval3dp(f2,u1,v1);
plot3d(x1,y1,z1);

xtitle('Twisted cylinder   ')


//#7 miobus strip
subplot(2,2,3)
st=.05;

function [x,y,z]=f2(u,v);
x=2*cos(v)+u.*cos(v/2);
y=2*sin(v)+u.*cos(v/2);
z=u.*sin(v/2);
endfunction
u1=-.5:st:.5+st;v1=0:st:2*pi+st;
[x1,y1,z1]=eval3dp(f2,u1,v1);
plot3d(x1,y1,z1);
xtitle('Miobus strip   ')
```

□

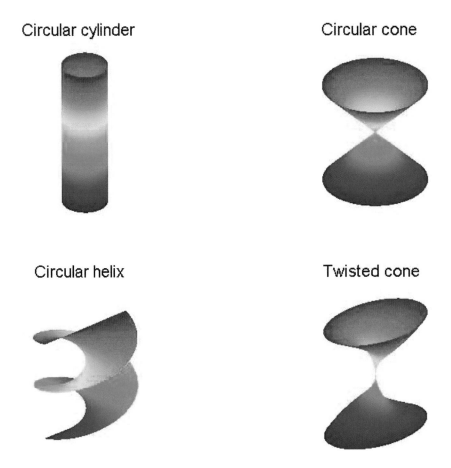

Figure 5.9: Parametric surfaces I

5.6 Homework: 3d Plots

5.6.1 *Graph the parametric curve*

$$x = \sin(t), \qquad y = \sin(2t), \qquad z = \sin(6t)$$

for $-2\pi \le t \le 2\pi$ *with step size* $.02\pi$ *and graph it.*

5.6.2 *Graph the parametric curve*

$$x = (1 + \cos 16t)\cos t, \qquad y = (1 + \cos 16t)\sin t, \qquad z = (1 + \cos 16t)$$

for $-2\pi \le t \le 2\pi$ *with step size* $.02\pi$ *and graph it.*

5.6.3 *Graph the surface by using fplot3d and rotate it*

$$z = -xye^{-(x^2 + y^2)}$$

on the square $[-3,3] \times [-3,3]$*. Draw the level curves using contour command.*

5.6.4 *Graph the dog saddle using fplot3d and rotate it*

$$z = xy^3 - yx^3$$

on the square $[-3,3] \times [-3,3]$*. Draw the level curves using contour command.*

5.6.5 *Graph the circular cylinder using plot3d and replot to generate three intersecting pipes with different colors*

$$x = \cos v; y = \sin v; z = u;$$

over the square $[-\pi,\pi] \times [-\pi,\pi]$ *with step size* 0.3*.*

5.6.6 *Plot the vector field* $(y,-x)$ *using champ1 function on the square* $[-2,2] \times [-2,2]$*.*

6 Applications

6.1 Calculus

Scilab has many built-in functions to perform numerical differentiation and integration with many options.

6.1.1 Differentiation

The linear approximation for first-order derivative of a given function $f(x)$ is given by

$$f'(x) \approx \frac{f(x+h) - f(x)}{h}$$

which is based on the following definition for small h:

$$f'(x) = \frac{df}{dx} = \lim_{h \to o} \left(\frac{f(x+h) - f(x)}{h} \right)$$

The command `diff` performs the first finite difference between the elements of any vector y:

$$diff(y) = \Delta y = y_{i+1} - y_i$$

6.1.1 *Plot the function* $y = x^3 - x$ *on the interval* $[-1.5, 1.5]$ *with 8 and 16 points and the corresponding first order derivatives using the* `diff` *function with bar graphs on 4 by 4 subplots.*

Solution:

```
// date and name
clear
x8=linspace(-1.5,1.5,8);
x16=linspace(-1.5,1.5,16);
y8=x8.^3-x8;
y16=x16.^3-x16;
slope8=diff(y8)./diff(x8);
slope16=diff(y16)./diff(x16);
x7=x8(1:7); //Adjust the x values for diff
x15=x16(1:15);
subplot(2,2,1)
plot(x8,y8,'-o')
xtitle('y=x^3-x')
```

92

```
subplot(2,2,2)
bar(x7,slope8)
xtitle('Slope of y=x^3-x' )
subplot(2,2,3)
plot(x16,y16,'-o')
xtitle('y=x^3-x')
subplot(2,2,4)
bar(x15,slope16)
xtitle('Slope of y=x^3-x' )
```

□

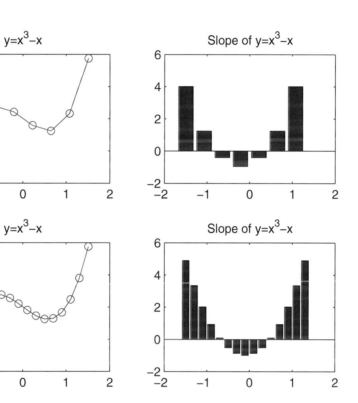

Figure 6.1: Example 1

6.1.2 *Plot the function $y = x\sin(x)$ on the interval $[-\pi, \pi]$ with 8 and 16 points and the corresponding derivatives using the* diff *function with bar graphs on 4 by 4 subplots.*

6.1.2 Numerical Integration

We can evaluate definite integrals of the form

$$I = \int_a^b f(x)\,dx$$

by methods of numerical integration which are called numerical quadrature, such as trapezoidal, Simpson formulas, and others. Scilab has a set of built-in functions to calculate the definite integrals;

intg(a, b, f)   evaluates the definite integral of a single variable function f over the interval $[a, b]$

intd2d(X,Y,f)   evaluates the double integral of a function f over 2D domain and X, Y are matrices of the vertices of the triangulation of the domain.

intd3d(X,Y,Z,f)   evaluates the 3D integral of a function f over 3D region and X, Y, Z are matrices of the vertices of the tetrahedron of the region.

The construction of the higher dimensional domains are not simple.

6.1.3 *Find*

$$I = \int_0^2 (3x^2 - 2x + 5)dx$$

Solution: *We know that the exact value of this integral is $I = x^3 - x^2 + 5x|_0^2 = (8 - 4 + 10) - (0) = 14$. The Scilab evaluation of this integral is entered as follows:*

```
function y=f(x),y=3*x^2-2*x+5;endfunction
exact=14;
I=intg(0,2,f)
abs(exact-I)
```
☐

6.1.4 *Find*

$$I_1 = \int_0^1 \cos(\pi t^2)dt$$

Solution:

```
function y=f(x),y=cos(%pi*x^2);endfunction
I=intg(0,1,f)

-->I=intg(0,1,f)
 I   =
     0.3739828
```
☐

6.1.5 *Compute the following two integrals and compare the result of the two functions by requesting the long format*

1. $q1 = \int_0^2 (\sqrt[3]{x + x^2})dx$

2. $q2 = \int_0^4 x\ln(x)dx$

Solution: *We can find the integral directly on the command window as follows*

```
function y=f(x),y=(x+x^2)^(1/3);endfunction
I=intg(0,2,f)
-->I1=intg(0,2,f)
 I1  =
    2.4175887
-->[I, e]=intg(0,2,f)
 e  =
     1.885D-09
 I  =
    2.4175887

function y=f(x),y=x*log(x);endfunction
I2=intg(0,4,f)
-->I2=intg(0,4,f)
 I2  =
    7.0903549
```

□

6.1.6 *Plot the function* $|\frac{sin(10x)}{x}|$ *over the interval* [0,2] *and find the area under this curve. Try to experiment with the convergence or divergence of this integral as you increase the upper bound toward infinity.*

Solution:

```
function y=f(x),y=abs(sin(10*x)/x) ;endfunction
I=intg(0,2,f)
-->I=intg(0,2,f)
 I  =
    3.0128756

x=linspace(%eps,2,200);
fplot2d(x,f)
xtitle('|sin(10*x)./x|')
```

□

6.1.7 *Approximate the area under the graph of* $y = 4 - x^2$ *and bounded by* $x = 0, x = 2$ *and the y-axis.*

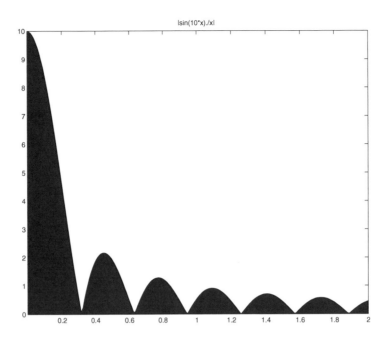

Figure 6.2: Area under a curve

6.1.8 *Compute the double integral $\int_0^1 \int_0^1 (yx^2 + xy^2) dy dx$*

Solution: *We need to triangulate the square into two triangles: ABC with vertices $A(0,0), B(1,0), C(1,1)$ and ACD with vertices $A(0,0), C(1,1), D(0,1)$. The double integration requires the construction of two matrices $X(3,2)$ of the abscissa of the vertices and $Y(3,2)$ of the ordinates of the vertices:*

```
function z=f(x,y);z=y*x^2+x*y^2 ;endfunction

X=[0,0;1,1;1,0]; // Abscissa of the vertices of ABC and ACD
Y=[0,0;0,1;1,1]; // Ordinates  of the vertices of ABC and ACD
//deff('z=f(x,y)','z=cos(x+y)')
[I,e]=int2d(X,Y,f)
// computes the integrand over the square [0 1]x[0 1]
-->[I,e]=int2d(X,Y,f)
 e  =
    7.401D-17
 I  =
    0.3333333
```

□

6.1.9 *Compute the double integral $\int_\pi^{2\pi} \int_0^\pi (y\sin(x) + x\cos(y)) dy dx$*

Solution: *We need to triangulate the rectangle into two triangles: ABC with vertices $A(\pi, 0), B(2\pi, 0), C(2\pi, \pi)$ and ACD with vertices $A(\pi, 0), C(2\pi, \pi), D(\pi, \pi)$. The double integration requires the construction of two matrices $X(3, 2)$ of the abscissa of the vertices and $Y(3, 2)$ of the ordinates of the vertices:*

```
function z=f(x,y);z=y*sin(x)+x*cos(y)  ;endfunction
X=[%pi,%pi;2*%pi,2*%pi;2*%pi,%pi];
Y=[0,0;0,%pi;%pi,%pi];
//deff('z=f(x,y)','z=cos(x+y)')
[I,e]=int2d(X,Y,f)
// the output
-->[I,e]=int2d(X,Y,f)
 e  =
    9.810D-11
 I  =
  - 9.8696044
```

6.1.3 Algebraic equations

We can solve algebraic equation $f(x) = 0$ by applying the function
`fsolve(x_0,'equation')  //x_0 initial guess`

6.1.10 *Find the solution of $sin(x) = e^x - 5$*

Solution: *We graph the equation $y = sin(x) - e^x + 5$, from the plot we guess the solution to be $x = 1$ corresponding to zero graph height. Use this value in the equation solver.*

```
x=-2:.01:2;y=sin(x)-exp(x)+5;plot(x,y)
function y=f(x);y=sin(x)-exp(x)+5  ;endfunction
x1=fsolve(1,f)
-->x1=fsolve(1,f)
 x1  =
    1.7878415
```

6.1.11 *Find the solution of the nonlinear algebraic equation $x^2 = 1 - tan(x)$.*

Solution: *We plot the equation $y = x^2 + tan(x) - 1$ over $[-1, 1]$, from the graph we guess the initial solution to be 0.5 which is used in the solution solver.*

```
x=-1:.01:1;y=x.^2+tan(x)-1;plot(x,y)
function y=f(x);y=x^2+tan(x)-1;  ;endfunction
x1=fsolve(0.5,f)
-->x1=fsolve(0.5,f)
 x1  =
    0.5832485
```

□

6.1.12 *Find all the real roots of the function $f(x) = x^3 - 4x^2 - 0.5x + 3.8$.*

6.1.13 *Find all the real roots of the function $g(x) = e^x - x - 1.9$.*

6.1.4 Differential Equations

Scilab has many functions for solving ordinary differential equations. These differential equation problems have the form

$$\frac{d}{dt}y(t) = f(t, y(t)), \quad y(t_0) = y_0$$

where

1. t is a real scalar over an interval such as $t = 0 : 0.01 : 12$

2. $y(t)$ is an unknown column vector.

3. t_0 initial time such as $t_0 = 0$ or

4. y_0 is an initial position (usually a vector).

The common Scilab ODE solver has the form

$$y = ode(y_0, t_0, t, f(t, y))$$

The ode solver has many options which are fully listed in Scilab Help. The main steps in Applying the ODE solver are

1. Solve for the derivative to identify the right hand side of the ode, that is $f(t, y)$

2. Define a function for the right hand side f

3. Define the interval for the solution: t

4. Specify the initial conditions t_0, y_0

5. Call the ODE solver and save the output: $y = ode(y_0, t_0, t, f)$

6. Plot the solution

7. Plot a vector field or phase plane as requested

First Order Differential Equations

6.1.14 *Solve the differential equation*

$$y' = -y\sin(2y) - \cos(x); \qquad y(0) = 1; \qquad x \in [0, 20]$$

Plot your solution.

Solution:

1. *Define the function of the right side:* $f(x, y) = -y\sin(2y) - \cos(x)$
2. *Vectorize the solution range:* x
3. *Identify the initial data:* $x0 = 0, y0 = 1$
4. *Call the ODE solver* ode(y0, x0, x, f) *and plot as follows*

```
function ydot=f(x,y); ydot=-y*sin(2*y)-cos(x); endfunction
x=0:0.05:20;
x0=0.0;
y0=1.0;
y=ode(y0,x0,x,f); plot(x,y,'b', 'thickness',3)
title (' Solution of dy/dx=ysin(2y)-cos(x)','fontsize', 3)
```

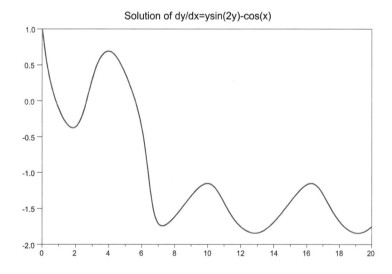

Figure 6.3: Example 1

□

6.1.15 *Plot the solutions of the differential equation* $\dfrac{dy}{dt} = y(1 - y) - sin(6t)$
on $t \in [0, 5]$ *for the following initial conditions*

1. $y(0) = 0.2$

2. $y(0) = 0.5$

3. $y(0) = 1.0$

4. $y(0) = 1.5$

*and draw a vector field using the **champ** command.*

> **Solution:** *Copy the following script to a file named* `ode1_solver.sce` *and run it.*

```
// Script file to solve a single first order DE
// with initial values
// dy/dt = y (1-y) -sin(6t) on 0<t<5
function ydot=f(t,y);
    ydot=y*(1-y)-sin(6*t);
endfunction
t=0:0.05:5;
t0=0;
y1=0.2;
y2=0.5;
y3=1.0;
y4=1.5;

y=ode(y1,t0,t,f); plot(t,y,'r')
y=ode(y2,t0,t,f); plot(t,y,'g')
y=ode(y3,t0,t,f); plot(t,y,'b')
y=ode(y4,t0,t,f); plot(t,y,'m')

///////////////////
//clf
t=0: .2: 5; y=-.5:.2:2;
function z=ft(t,y),z=1;endfunction
function z=fy(t,y),z=y*(1-y)-sin(6*t);endfunction
zt=feval(t,y,ft); zy=feval(t,y,fy);
champ1(t,y,zt,zy)

xtitle('dy/dt= y(1-y)-sin(6t)')
```

$\square$

6.1.16 *Plot the solution of the first order, nonlinear differential equation*

$$y' = \frac{y^3 \sin(3x)}{x^2}$$

with initial condition $y(1) = 2$ on the interval $[1,10]$.

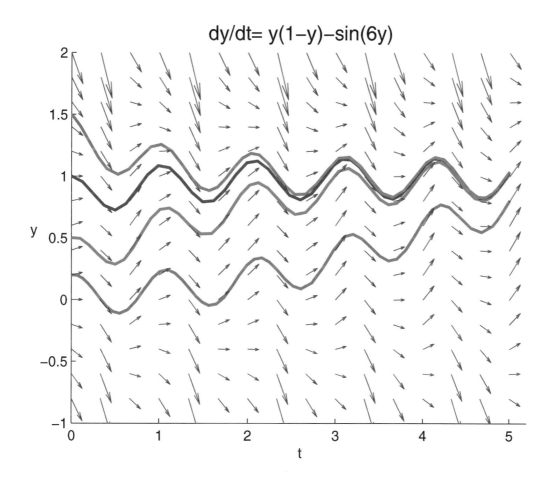

Figure 6.4: Example 2

Second Order Differential Equations

Higher order differential equations must be reduced to a system of first order differential equations. This can be achieved by introducing a set of new variables.

Reduction of higher-order equations to first-order systems

To write the second order equation

$$x^{''} + x = \sin t$$

We introduce new variables $u_1 = x, u_2 = x'$ and solve for $x'' = -x + \sin t$, this will be rewritten as first-order system as follows

$$u_1' = u_2$$
$$u_2' = -u_1 + \sin t$$

6.1.17 *Express the second order equation as a first-order system of equation*

$$2y'' + 6y' - 8y = 9\cos 2t$$

Solution: *Introduce new variables* $u_1 = y, u_2 = y'$ *and solve for* $y'' = -3y' + 4u_1 + 4.5\cos 2t$, *so that*

$$u_1' = u_2$$
$$u_2' = -3u_2 + 4u_1 + 4.5\cos 2t$$

□

6.1.18 *Express the second order equation as a first-order system of equation*

$$x''' - x^2 x'' + 5x'^3 = \sin t$$

Solution: *Introduce new variables* $u_1 = x, u_2 = x', u_3 = x''$ *and solve for* $x''' = x^2 x'' - 5x'^3 + \sin t$, *so that*

$$u_1' = u_2$$
$$u_2' = u_3$$
$$u_3' = u_1^2 u_3 - 5u_2^3 + \sin t$$

□

6.1.19 *Plot the solution of the damped motion*

$$x'' + x' + 4x = 0$$

with initial condition $x(0) = 2, x'(0) = 3$ *over the interval* $[0, 12]$ *and draw the phase plane with vector field.*

Solution:

We introduce new variables $u_1 = x, u_2 = x'$ *and solve for* $x'' = -x' - 4x$, *this will be rewritten as first-order system as follows*

$$u_1' = u_2$$
$$u_2' = -u_2 - 4u_1$$

```
// Script file to solve a 2 by 2 first order system of DE
// with initial values
// x"=-x'-4x on 0<t<12

function [udr]=damp(t,y);
    ud1=y(2); ud2=-y(2)-4*y(1);
    udr=[ud1;ud2];
endfunction
t=0:.1:12;
t0=0;
```

```
u1=[2;3];
[sol]=ode(u1,t0,t,damp);
subplot(2,1,1)
plot(t,sol(1,:),'b','thickness',3)
xtitle('The position of motion','Time', 'x(t)')


subplot(2,1,2)
plot(sol(1,:),sol(2,:),'r','thickness',3)
xtitle('Phase Plane', 'Position', 'Velocity')

z1 = linspace(-1.5,2.5,15);
z2 = linspace(-4,3,15);
fchamp(damp,0,z1,z2) // Draw vector field
```

☐

6.1.20 *Plot the solution of the forced motion*

$$x'' + x = \sin t$$

with initial condition $x(0) = 2, x'(0) = 1$ over the interval $[0,10]$ and draw the phase plane with vector field.

6.1.21 *Write a code to plot three solutions of the pendulum equation*

$$\frac{d^2 y(t)}{dt^2} + 0.25 \frac{dy(t)}{dt} + \sin(y) = 0; \qquad t \in [0, 20]$$

and draw a vector field.

> **Solution:**   *We rewrite the second order equation as a system of first order equations by introducing new variables*
>
> $$y1 = y, \qquad y2 = \frac{dy}{dt}, \qquad \frac{dy_2}{dt} = \frac{d^2 y(t)}{dt^2}$$
>
> *as follows:*
> $$\frac{dy_1}{dt} = y_2; \qquad \frac{dy_2}{dt} = -0.25 y_2 - \sin(y_1)$$
>
> *Save the following script in a file named* ode2_solver.sce *and run it.*

```
// Script file to solve a 2 by 2 first order system of DE
// with initial values
// y'' = -.25y'-sin(y) on 0<t<20


function [ydot]=pend(t,y);..
```

```
        yd1=y(2);yd2=-0.25*y(2) -sin( y(1));..
        ydot=[yd1; yd2 ]; endfunction

//or
//deff("[xdot] = pend(t,x)",..
//          ["xd1 = x(2)";..
//            "xd2 = -0.25*x(2) -sin (x(1))";..
//            "xdot = [ xd1 ; xd2 ]"]);

t=0:.2:20;
x0=[-5 ; -2]; t0=0;
[sol]=ode(x0,t0,t,pend);
plot(sol(1,:), sol(2,:), 'r' )
x2=[5;-2];
[sol]=ode(x2,t0,t,pend);
plot(sol(1,:), sol(2,:), 'g' )
x4=[-4.;3];
[sol]=ode(x4,t0,t,pend);
plot(sol(1,:), sol(2,:), 'b' )


x5=[4;-3];
[sol]=ode(x5,t0,t,pend);
plot(sol(1,:), sol(2,:), 'm' )



xf=linspace(-8, 8, 20); yf=linspace(-3, 3, 10);
fchamp(pend, 0, xf, yf);


xtitle ('The Pendulum: Phase Diagram with 4 trajectories')
```

□

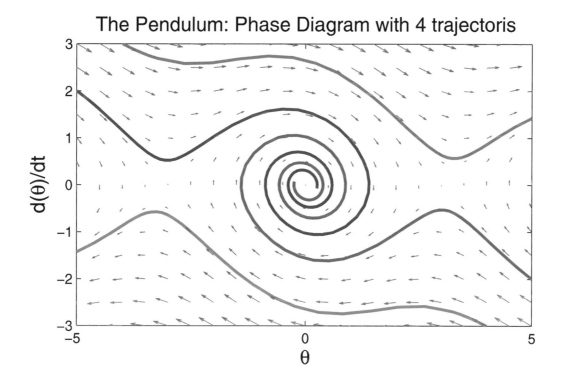

Figure 6.5: Example 4

6.2 Homework: Integration, Algebraic and Differential Equations

6.2.1 *Compute the following integrals using Scilab integration functions (intg, int2d, int3d):*

1.

$$\int_2^3 x^3 \sin(x^2)\,dx$$

2.

$$\int_{-2}^2 \int_{-2}^2 \frac{1}{x^2 + y^2}\,dx\,dy$$

6.2.2 *Find the solutions of the equation $e^{-x^2} + 0.1(x-1)^2 - 0.5 = 0$ by using the scilab command fsolve. Hint to choose an initial guess, graph the equation and visually select good starting guess.*

6.2.3 *Solve the first order differential equation* $\dfrac{dy}{dx} = \dfrac{y}{x} + x\cos x$ *on the interval* $[1,25]$ *with initial condition* $y(1) = 0$

6.2.4 *Plot the solution of the forced motion*

$$x'' + 4x' + 4x = \cos 2t$$

with initial condition $x(0) = 1, x'(0) = -2$ *over the interval* $[0,20]$ *and draw the phase plane with vector field.*

6.2.5 *Solve the second order differential equation* $\dfrac{dx^2}{dt^2} + 25x = \sin(5.5t)$ *on the interval* $[0,30]$ *and with initial condition* $x(0) = 0, x'(0) = 0$. *Hint rewrite the equation as a system of equation that is*

$$\frac{dy_1}{dt} = y_2; \qquad \frac{dy_2}{dt} = -25y_1 + \sin(5.5t)$$

and use the pendulum script to plot the phase plane and the solution on different figures.

Solution:

```
function [ydot]=rside(t,y);..
    yd1=y(2);yd2=-25*y(1) +sin( 5.5*t);..
    ydot=[yd1; yd2 ];
    endfunction

subplot(2,1,1)
t=0:.02:30;
x0=[0 ; 0]; t0=0;
[sol]=ode(x0,t0,t,rside);
plot(sol(1,:), sol(2,:), 'r' )
subplot(2,1,2)
plot(t,sol(1,:))
```

$\square$

6.2.6 *Solve the second order differential equation* $\dfrac{dx^2}{dt^2} + 0.5\dfrac{dx}{dt} + 25x = \sin(5t)$ *on the interval* $[0,30]$ *and with initial condition* $x(0) = 1, x'(0) = 1$. *Plot the phase plane and the solution on different figures.*
    Hint for the right side:

```
function [ydot]=rside(t,y);
    yd1=y(2);yd2=-.5*y(2) -25*y(1)+sin( 5*t);
    ydot=[yd1; yd2 ];
    endfunction
```

| 7 | Scilab Problem Sets

7.1 Arithmetic

7.1.1 *Type the following into Scilab at the prompt command* $-->$

1. $4 - 5 * 6$

2. $3.45 * (-9.1)/3.27$

3. 3.05^3

4. $4^{(4^4)}$

5. $\sqrt{121}$

6. $\sin(pi/2)$

7. $12 * 4/2 * 12/3$

8. $3 \wedge (2 + 3)$

9. $(-3)^2 - \dfrac{5}{5 + 10}$

10. $\dfrac{4^{3-2} - 3}{8 - 3}$

11. $\sqrt{9 + 3^7}$

7.1.2 *Use Scilab to define and compute the following*

1. *Define the array* $x = [1.1 \quad 2.2 \quad 3.3 \quad 5]$

2. *Find the cosine of* x

3. *Subtract* 1.1 *from each element of* x

4. *Define array* $y = [1 \quad 2 \quad 3 \quad 4]$

5. *Add the elements of* x *to the corresponding elements of* y

6. *Multiply each element of* x *by corresponding elements of* y

7. *Cube each element* y

8. *Define a matrix* z *of even numbers from* 0 *to* 20

9. Use the linspace *function to define an array **v** of all values between 3 and 12*

7.1.3 *Compute the area of the circle* $A = \pi r^2$ *with* $r = [1 \quad 3 \quad \pi]$

7.1.4 *Define a vector with values from* **0** *to* 2π *with increments of* $\pi/20$

7.1.5 *Define a vector with evenly spaced values from* **5** *to* **100** *with increments of* **15**

7.1.6 *The distance of freely falling object is given by* $d = \frac{1}{2}gt^2$ *where* $g = 9.8m/s^2$. *Construct a table of time versus distance for the first 10 seconds.*

7.2   Basic Functions

7.2.1 *Use help menu to read how to use the functions*

1. *sin*

2. *tan*

3. *exp*

4. *ln*

5. *arctan*

6. *sqrt*

7. *abs*

7.2.2 *Create a vector **x** from* **−10** *to* **10** *with an increment of* **1**

1. *Find the square root of the vector*

2. *Find the absolute value of the vector*

3. *Find* e^x

4. *Find* $\ln(x)$ *and* $\log_{10}(x)$

5. *Divide **x** by* **−3**

6. *Find the remainder of **x** divided by* **2**

7.2.3 *Using Scilab*

1. *Factor* **729**. *Use* factor

2. *Approximate π as a rational number. Use* rats

3. *Approximate e as a rational number*

4. *Find* **6!** *and* **60!**. *Use* factorial

7.2.4 *Calculate the following*

1. $\cos(3\theta)$ *for* $\theta = \pi/4$

2. $\sin(2\theta)$ *for* $0 \le \theta \le 2\pi$ *with step size* 0.2π

3. *Find* $\cos^{-1}(.5)$

7.2.5 *Using* rand *functions, compute the following*

1. *Create* 3×3 *matrix of uniformly distributed random values*

2. *Create* 3×3 *matrix of normally distributed random values*

7.3 Scilab Matrices

7.3.1 *Given the matrices*

$$a = \begin{bmatrix} 10 & 14 & 0 & 1 \end{bmatrix}, b = \begin{bmatrix} 2 & 5 & 8 \\ 4 & 1 & -2 \\ 6 & 3 & 0 \end{bmatrix}, c = \begin{bmatrix} 20 \\ 10 \\ 1 \end{bmatrix}$$

1. *Assign to $x1$ the second column of a*

2. *Assign to $x2$ the first column of b*

3. *Assign to $x3$ the third row of b*

4. *Assign to $x4$ the diagonal of b*

5. *Assign to $x5$ the second column of a and c*

7.3.2 *Using* zeros ones diag *functions, compute the following*

1. *Create* 4×4 *matrix of zeros*

2. *Create* 2×4 *matrix of zeros*

3. *Create* 3×3 *matrix of ones*

4. *Create* 5×4 *matrix of 6*

5. *Create* 4×4 *matrix of zeros*

6. *Create* 4×4 *matrix whose diagonal is* $1, 2, 3, 4$

7.4 Scilab Plots

7.4.1   1. *Plot x versus $y1 = \sin(15x)\sin(3x)$ on the interval $0 \le x \le 2\pi$ in increments of 0.1π.*

2. *Add a title and labels to the plot*

3. *Let $y2 = 2\cos(x)$. Plot x versus $y1$ and $y2$ on $0 \le x \le 2\pi$*

7.4.2   1. *Divide a figure into two rows and one column*

2. *In the top part, plot $y = \tanh(2x)$ on the interval $-4 \le x \le 4$ in increments of 0.1.*

3. *Add a title and labels to the plot*

4. *In the bottom, plot x versus $y = \tan(x)$ on the same range*

5. *Add a title and labels to the plot*

6. *repeat the plots on vertical division of the figure*

7.4.3 *Plot the functions $y1 = \sin(x), y2 = \sin(2x), y3 = \sin(3x)$ on $-\pi$ to π*

1. *Plot $y1$ in red and solid*

2. *Plot $y2$ in blue and dashed*

3. *Plot $y3$ in green and dotted*

7.4.4 *Create a vector x from 0 to 30π with step size $.1\pi$. Let $y = x\sin(2x), z = x\cos(2x)$*

1. *Plot x versus y*

2. *Create a polar plot of x versus y*

3. *Create a 3-d plot of x, y, z with a title and labels*

7.4.5 *Let*
$$Z = \cos(\sqrt{X^2 + Y^2})$$

1. *Use plot3d to create 3d plot for Z*

2. *Generate a contour plot of Z*

7.4.6 *Create Scilab function to evaluate*

1. *$y(x) = x^3$*

2. *$y = e^{-x^2}$*

7.5 Scilab Algebra

7.5.1 *Find the dot product of the vectors*

$$A = \begin{bmatrix} 2 & 0 & -3 & 5 \end{bmatrix}, B = \begin{bmatrix} 6 & -6 & -3 & 3 \end{bmatrix}$$

7.5.2 *Find the product of the matrices*

$$A = \begin{bmatrix} 2 & 4 & 6 \\ 5 & 3 & 1 \end{bmatrix}, B = \begin{bmatrix} -1 & 1 \\ 0 & 2 \\ 3 & -1 \end{bmatrix} \text{ and show that } A*B \neq B*A$$

7.5.3 *Given the matrix* $A = \begin{bmatrix} 3 & -1 \\ 4 & 2 \end{bmatrix}$,

1. *Raise A to second power*

2. *Compute the determinant of A*

3. *Compute the inverse of A*

7.5.4 *Solve the system of linear equations*

$3x + 4y - z = 10$

$2x - y + 2z = 2$

$x - 4y + 3z = 8$

7.6 Problem Sets

7.6.1 *Compute to 15 digits*

1. $\sinh(0.5)$, *and* $\cosh(0.5)$

2. $\ln(10)$

3. *arctan(10)*

7.6.2 *Solve the system*

$$x + 4y - z = 1$$

$$2x - 4y + 5z = -2$$

$$3x + 3y + 10z = 2$$

7.6.3 *Use* fsolve *to solve the equations as appropriate:*

1. $7x - 52 = 0$, *numerical solution to 17 digits*

2. $e^{-x} = -5x + 4$

7.6.4 *Use* contour *to do the following:*

1. *Plot the level curves of the function* $f(x,y) = 2x^2 - 2y^2 - 3x^3 + 3y^3$ *in the square between* -1 *and* 1. *Describe the behavior o the surface near zero and in the larger region*

2. *Plot the level curves of the function* $f(x,y) = x\ln y - y\ln x$ *that contains the point* (e, e)

7.6.5 *Compute the integrals:*

1. $\int_0^{2\pi} e^{\cos x} dx$

2. $\int_0^1 \sqrt{x^3 + 4} dx$

7.6.6 *Plot the surfaces :*

1. $z = \cos x \cos y$, *for* $-5\pi \le x \le 5\pi$, $-5\pi \le y \le 5\pi$

2. $z = (x^2 + y^2)\sin(x^2 + y^2)$, *for* $-2 \le x \le 2$, $-2 \le y \le 2$

7.6.7 *Plot the three dimensional curve* $x = e^{-t}\cos(t), y = e^{-t}\sin(t), z = t - 10$ *over* $0 \le t \le 20$.

7.6.8 *Use Scilab to solve* $5x^3 - 3x^2 = 2x$.

7.6.9 *Plot the three dimensional curve*

$$x = \cos t, \qquad y = \sin t, \qquad z = \sin 2t$$

for $0\pi \le t \le 2\pi$ *with a spacing of* $.01\pi$.

7.6.10 *Let*

$$f(x, y) = \frac{x^2 - 2y^2}{x^4 + 2y^2}$$

Graph the surface $f(x, y)$

7.6.11 *A parametrization of Umbilic Torus is given by*

$$x = [7 + \cos(\tfrac{1}{3}s - 2t) + 2\cos(\tfrac{1}{3}s + 2t)] \sin s$$

$$y = [7 + \cos(\tfrac{1}{3}s - 2t) + 2\cos(\tfrac{1}{3}s + 2t)] \cos s$$

$$z = \sin(\tfrac{1}{3}s - 2t) + 2\sin(\tfrac{1}{3}s + 2t)$$

Graph this torus on the square $-\pi \le s \le \pi$, $-\pi \le t \le \pi$.

7.6.12 *Given the two polynomial functions:*

$$f(x) = -4x^2 + 2x + 3$$

$$g(x) = x^4 - 4$$

Answer the following

1. *Plot the two functions and find their intersection points.*

2. *Find the area of the region between the two functions interior to the two intersection points.*

3. *Find the area of the region formed by* $f(x)$ *above the x-axis.*

4. *Find the area of the region formed by* $g(x)$ *below the x-axis.*

7.6.13 *Solve the first order differential equation* $e^x y' - y^2 = x$ *on the interval* $[0, 10]$ *with initial condition* $y(0) = 2$

7.6.14 *Plot the solution of the second order differential equation*

$$x'' + 25x = \sin 5.4t$$

with initial condition $x(0) = 0, x'(0) = 0$ *over the interval* $[0, 30]$ *and draw the phase plane. The displayed solution is an example of the beat phenomenon.*

Made in the USA
Lexington, KY
21 November 2013